THE POWER OF MOVING ON

THE POWER OF MOVING ON

HOW TO LET GO AND LIVE
THE LIFE YOU WANT

JOHN PURKISS

(SRI NITHYA BANAHASTANANDA)

monoray

First published in Great Britain in 2025 by Monoray,
an imprint of Octopus Publishing Group Ltd
Carmelite House 50 Victoria Embankment
London EC4Y 0DZ
www.octopusbooks.co.uk

An Hachette UK Company
www.hachette.co.uk

The authorized representative in the EEA is Hachette Ireland,
8 Castlecourt Centre, Dublin 15, D15 XTP3, Ireland (email: info@hbgi.ie)

Distributed in the US by Hachette Book Group
1290 Avenue of the Americas, 4th and 5th Floors
New York, NY 10104

Distributed in Canada by Canadian Manda Group
664 Annette St., Toronto, Ontario, Canada M6S 2C8

ISBN 978-1-80096-360-3
eBook ISBN 978-1-80096-361-0

A CIP catalogue record for this book is available from the British Library.

Typeset in 10.25/14.5pt MinionPro by Six Red Marbles UK,
Thetford, Norfolk.

Printed and bound in Great Britain.

1 3 5 7 9 10 8 6 4 2

This FSC® label means that materials used for
the product have been responsibly sourced.

This monoray book was crafted and published by Jake Lingwood,
Jessica Minocha, Rimsha Falak, Mel Four and Sarah Parry.

This book does not constitute professional advice.

The information this book contains is not intended to take the place of treatment by a qualified medical practitioner; always consult a medical professional. This book also contains references to themes of suicide. Please seek professional services if you are affected by this content. Although the publisher and author have used their reasonable efforts in preparing this book, no representations or warranties are made with respect to the accuracy or completeness of the contents of this book and any implied warranties of satisfactory quality or fitness for purpose are excluded. The publisher is not engaged in rendering professional services and neither the publisher nor the author shall be liable for damages arising herefrom. The services of a competent professional should be sought if professional advice or other expert assistance is required.

CONTENTS

FOR THE CREATOR IN ALL OF US

INTRODUCTION

IT'S TIME TO MOVE ON

What do you want to happen in your life? Do you want more money? Are you looking for a new relationship? Is poor health holding you back? Maybe you have the health, wealth and relationships you want, but you feel your life lacks purpose. One way or another, most of us feel stuck.

In my previous book, *The Power of Letting Go*, I showed how to:

- **Let go of thoughts**
- **Let go of pain**
- **Let go completely**

The Power of Moving On is another big step forward. Now that you've discovered the power of letting go, I'm going to turn your attention to what you want. Moving on is more than letting go of the past – it's about changing your approach to life. I'm going to show you how to move on to a much more effective way of manifesting your true desires – whether it's health, wealth or relationships. It'll be much easier for you to lead a fulfilling life.

When I talk about manifesting I'm describing how to bring your desires into physical existence. It's simple but profound. The techniques in this book will enable you to manifest:

- **Effectively**
- **Consciously**
- **Consistently**

You're going to take a big step – from experiencing the world as an individual to a higher level of being. Once you start manifesting your desires in this way, you'll feel very different – as I do. You'll hold a desire inside you until it materializes. You may or may not need to take action. If you do take action, your intuition will tell you what to do, moment by moment. You can relax in the knowledge that you're doing the right thing at the right time. Your desires will manifest much more easily – often in ways you never imagined.

In order to experience this profound change, you need to turn inwards and work on yourself. Because when our inner world changes, the outer world changes automatically.

Let's acknowledge our starting point. If something isn't working in our lives, most of us look for an *external* solution: we try to fix our bodies, or the people around us, or the situation in which we find ourselves. If our health is poor, we change our diet, get more exercise or seek medical treatment. If a relationship is deteriorating, we talk to the other person and try to sort things out. If our career isn't going the way we want, we work harder or search for another opportunity. If we don't have enough money, we look for ways to acquire more of it.

Many of us also *label* other people and the world around us. For example, we say that s/he is an idiot or a narcissist, or the economy is in crisis, or our society is broken. We say that other people are the problem – and then we try to fix them.

Eventually, we reach the point of exhaustion, overwhelm or despair. Then what?

It's time to question our assumptions

Most of us have made two major assumptions – unconsciously – as a result of our social conditioning:

1. **I'm separate from other people and the world around me.**
2. **My life is governed by the laws of classical physics.**

Let's start with the first assumption. Most of us have been conditioned to believe that we're just a body and a mind – which I'll call the body/mind. There are billions of other body/minds and we're all separate. We're all trying to get what we want and avoid what we don't want. This leads to a huge amount of stress as we bump into each other, trying to outsmart or manipulate each other, occasionally attacking each other.

The assumption that we're separate body/minds pervades our culture. In economics it's the person who tries to maximize his or her economic wellbeing – otherwise known as *utility*. Finance and marketing have adopted a similar approach, with a focus on the individual. Psychology and medicine are also based on the concept of people being separate from one another.

The assumption that we're separate leads to situations that we can observe in daily life. For example:

- **We try to control other people.**
- **We look for our 'other half' in the hope of feeling whole.**
- **We're violent towards other people and animals.**
- **We damage our environment, assuming it's separate from us.**

This brings us to the second assumption: that our lives are governed by the laws of classical physics. In 1687 Sir Isaac Newton published a book commonly referred to as the *Principia.*[1] It states the first three laws of motion and the principle of universal gravitation. This is the basis of the physics that most of us were taught at school. One underlying principle is that, if we apply a particular force to an object, the outcome is highly predictable.

If we assume we're separate body/minds in a world governed by classical physics, the only way to make things happen is to take action with our bodies – or persuade someone else to do so. This includes our family, friends, colleagues, clients, customers – everyone.

When other people don't cooperate, we may get stressed and feel powerless, then grit our teeth and keep working away – trying to cajole other people so we get what we want. It's a recipe for exhaustion.

If you're making a big effort but not achieving the results you want, it's time to question your assumptions. Wrong assumptions lead to wrong conclusions: garbage in, garbage out.

If you're working hard while making these assumptions, then here are the sorts of things you'll notice in your life:

- **You're making a big effort with little or no result.**
- **You feel as though you're going backwards.**
- **You feel stressed.**
- **Other people avoid you.**
- **You feel bad about yourself.**

It's time to look inwards

This brings us to the Vedic tradition. *Veda* is a Sanskrit word which means 'knowledge'. The word 'science' is derived from the Latin word *scientia*, which also means 'knowledge'. However, there's a key difference between the Vedic and scientific approaches. Science emphasizes *looking outwards* to acquire knowledge – for example, by conducting experiments in a laboratory. By contrast, the Vedic tradition emphasizes *looking inwards* to acquire knowledge. This approach can still be empirical: in other words, based on observation and experience. Once a principle has been formulated, other people can test it to see if they have a similar experience.

In this book I'm going to share techniques that have worked for me and many others, as I did in *The Power of Letting Go*. Since it was published I've had the opportunity to go even deeper into the subject, as I'll describe in this book. I'm also going to explain letting go on a whole new level. I'll help you to have your own experiences – and manifest your desires much more easily.

Why aren't you manifesting all your desires already?

It's highly likely that you're using your mind and body to try to manifest your desires. In other words, you're thinking a lot and taking lots of action. You're behaving as though you're a separate body/mind in a world governed by the laws of classical physics. You may be visualizing the desired outcome, or writing down affirmations, and then taking lots of action – but it still isn't working. There are only so many hours in the day, and there's only so much pressure you can put on other people to get them to do what you want – whether it's your partner, a family member or a colleague.

At this point you may be asking: why aren't I manifesting my desires? But you *are* manifesting some of them, otherwise you wouldn't be alive, reading this book. You have a desire to live and you have a desire to read this book.

However, there are some desires that you *aren't* manifesting. There are also things that you *don't* want to happen, but they happen anyway. I'm going to show you that you aren't a powerless victim of circumstance. You're just manifesting unconsciously, that's all.

What's happening in your life reflects what's happening *inside* you. If you turn inwards and attend to yourself consciously, things will change. I'm going to show you how to manifest all your desires consciously – including health, wealth and relationships.

Let's go back to what you want to happen in your life. What do you want to move from and to? This book will show you how.

Many of us are in the habit of thinking a lot. We assume we have to work hard to achieve anything. We also get stressed. When we do this, we're relying on our mind, which has its limitations. The mind is just a bunch of thoughts.

It's time to move on from the mind to the intelligence that's running the cosmos, including your body and the world around you. If you tune into this Cosmic Intelligence, your desires will be fulfilled much more easily. The Sanskrit term for Cosmic Intelligence is *Paramashiva.*[2]

Then there's the bigger picture. In the world around us there's a lot of violence and environmental destruction – which we say we don't want. But what can we do about this situation? The techniques I'm going to show you will reduce the violence *in you.* This will directly affect everyone around you – and the whole world.

It's important to note that I didn't invent the teachings in this book. They go back many thousands of years. Unless otherwise stated, I learned them from SPH Sri Nithyananda Paramashivam, known to his followers as *Swamiji.* My role is to express them in plain English – with a few diagrams. I'll explain each principle and describe my experiences, some of which you may find surprising.

There are also exercises to help you have your own experiences. When you do these exercises, please use a pen and paper – it will be much more effective than a keyboard and a screen. There's also space at the back of this book for you to make notes.

Let's get started.

SUMMARY

- Most of us struggle in at least one area of our lives.
- If something isn't working, we tend to look for an *external* solution.
- Most of us have made two major assumptions: (1) I'm a separate body/mind, (2) My life is governed by the laws of classical physics. If you're making a big effort but not achieving the results you want, it's time to question your assumptions.
- Science emphasizes *looking outwards* to acquire knowledge – for example, by conducting experiments in a laboratory – while the Vedic tradition emphasizes *looking inwards* to acquire knowledge.
- It's highly likely that you're using your mind and body to manifest your desires – but it may not be working very well.
- You're already manifesting some of your desires, but you may be doing so unconsciously. I'm going to show you how to manifest all your desires consciously – including health, wealth and relationships.
- The solution is to tune into the Cosmic Intelligence.

1

KNOW YOUR DESIRES

ARE YOU LIVING THE LIFE YOU WANT?

Do you even know what you want?

Please take a pen and paper. Write down what you want to happen in three main areas of your life:

1. **Health**
2. **Wealth**
3. **Relationships**

Now let me ask you a question: are you sure *you're* the one who wants these things? Maybe your parents have always wanted you to do a particular job. Maybe you're expected to go to university – or *not* go to university. Maybe you're expected to be wealthy or poor – or married or single – just like the people around you.

You may have been complying with social norms for years. Now it's time to ask yourself what you really want.

Maybe you're more concerned about what you *don't* want. This is particularly common in the area of relationships. We have a relationship that doesn't work out the way we hoped, so we decide to avoid 'that kind of person' in future. If we focus on what we don't want, we're likely to get more of it.

Many of us have a lot of fear. We're afraid that we won't manifest what we want – or we'll keep manifesting what we don't want. Or both.

I'm going to show you how to let go of fear and live the life you want. Please write down your desires without worrying about how risky it may be, or what people will think of you. I'll show you later how to let go of the fear, so it bothers you less and less.

DISCOVER YOUR TRUE DESIRES

In order to identify your true desires, you can start by removing the other desires, which fall into four categories:

- **Borrowed desires, otherwise known as wants**
- **Complicating desires**
- **Conflicting desires**
- **Contradicting desires**

1. Borrowed desires

You may want something because other people want it. For example, you want a Ferrari because your brother wants a Ferrari. Or you want to have children because your friends want children.

You may also start wanting something because of expectations from your family. Some people feel external pressure to become a doctor or an engineer because it's seen as a good job. Others want to get married at a certain age due to family expectations.

We also borrow desires from society as a whole. The media constantly tells us about someone's glamorous lifestyle, or some other person's ascent of Mount Kilimanjaro. Frequently, the aim is to get us to spend money on all kinds of products and services so we can post them on social media – and so the cycle continues.

We feel bad about ourselves, so we unconsciously adopt someone else's desire, assuming that fulfilling it will make us feel better about ourselves. Soon we're on a hamster wheel, pursuing borrowed desires to alleviate our pain.

Pursuing borrowed desires is a distraction and will leave you feeling dissatisfied. Recognizing and dropping borrowed desires will allow you to follow your unique path.

2. Complicating desires

Complicating desires are those that lead to more complications instead of resolving an issue. Here's an example. Let's imagine you have a desire to write a book. In order to do this, you decide to take a writing course. Maybe you enrol for a degree in English Literature or even a master's degree in writing. You pile one desire on top of another. The whole thing becomes complicated – and your original desire is pushed further and further out of reach.

Alternatively, you could decide on the book you're going to write, then gather whatever information you need to make it happen. You can apply this approach to any activity. I've met people who want to start a business, and assume they need to study accounting, finance, law, marketing and technology. Instead, you can work with people who already have some of the knowledge you need.

Many of us make assumptions about the steps required to manifest our desires. We think a lot instead of tuning into the Cosmic Intelligence. It may seem logical that we need to do A, B and C in order to arrive at D, but life isn't logical. Once we're clear about what we're manifesting, we can let go and allow it to happen in unexpected ways. I'll show you how this works.

3. Conflicting desires

Conflicting desires are when you have two opposing desires. One example is wanting to go out for the day, and simultaneously wanting to stay at home. Another example is wanting to build a big business while simultaneously wanting to relax on the beach all day. Pursuing one desire may hinder another. It's essential to recognize and reconcile these conflicts. Then you can stay focused.

4. Contradicting desires

A contradicting desire is when you wish for something, but your actions or intentions contradict that wish. One example is wanting to lose weight, but overeating. Your conscious desire to lose weight is contradicted by unconscious habits or beliefs that lead to overeating.

Identify your true desires

Please make a list of all your desires, using a pen and paper. Then look inwards and visualize each of them, one by one. Notice how you feel. Next to each desire, make a note of whether it's borrowed, conflicting, complicating or contradicting – or none of those. Through this process, you can discover the desires that are truly yours – your true desires. Only these desires are worth fulfilling.

HOW DESIRES MANIFEST

Here's a common trap that many people fall into:

- **You think about how you can make something happen.**
- **You fail to come up with an answer.**
- **You then conclude it's impossible.**

Just because your mind can't figure it out right now doesn't mean it can't happen. What if the Wright Brothers had come to that conclusion about air travel?

Here's another example. Imagine you want to spend the summer in a European city, but hotels and rented apartments are too expensive. Your mind can't figure out a solution. Then a friend of a friend invites you to stay in their house free of charge while they're away. All you have to do is keep an eye on the property, mow the lawn and feed their pet.

It's best to keep an open mind about *how* your desires are going to manifest. The intelligence that runs the cosmos will take care of that. I'll show you how it works.

Choose your words carefully

As I'll explain in this book, the cosmos responds to your thoughts, words and actions. If you declare, 'Let me manifest X', the cosmos says *tathastu* – 'so be it' – and your desire starts to materialize.

But if you say 'I *want* to create X', the cosmos may say 'so be it', and you'll carry on wanting. The cosmos has given you exactly what you declared.

When you say 'Let me manifest X,' you're taking responsibility for the manifestation, aligning it with your conscious intention. For example, you might say, 'Let me manifest a successful business'.

At this point your mind might tell you it's impossible, you're not good enough or you don't have the right experience. I'm going to show you how to remove these and other negative thought patterns. You'll become more and more confident about manifesting.

I often declare what I'm manifesting when I have no idea *how* it's going to happen. The Cosmic Intelligence takes care of that – as I'll explain.

When appropriate, you can tell other people what you're manifesting.

I've often heard recommendations that you shouldn't tell people what you're manifesting, in case they pour cold water on your idea and put you off. This assumes you suffer from self-doubt. To be fair, that's true for many people. The exercises in this book will show you any pain patterns that may be causing self-doubt in you. I'll show you how to remove them.

My experience is that selectively telling people what I'm working on can be extremely helpful. They often contribute ideas or contacts that help to make it happen. One example is Anne Boden, who kept telling people, 'I'm starting a bank'. Within a few years, Starling Bank had a valuation in the billions of pounds.

Visualize your desires

The process I'm going to describe in this book is so powerful that it doesn't require deliberate visualization. However, I do recommend that you explore your desire visually.

For example, if you're planning to work, live or study somewhere, you can go there and walk around. Your desire will become something you can see and touch. If you want to manifest a physical object, you can go to a place where it's on sale – or otherwise available – then see and touch it.

Your desires are likely to evolve

As you explore a desire, it may change in some way. For example, you might want to start your own business. Over a period of time you learn about different types of business and become clearer about what you want to manifest. You also raise the level of your consciousness – with the help of this book – and become more confident about manifesting your desires. Don't be surprised if your vision expands and becomes far more ambitious in any area of your life.

Once you're clear about your desire, stay focused

Imagine you're using a magnifying glass to focus the sun's rays on a piece of paper, so it catches fire. If you keep moving the magnifying glass around, nothing will happen. If you hold it steady in one place, at some point the paper will catch fire and start burning out of control.

If you stay focused on what you're manifesting, the cosmos will align with that and support your intention. It will show you new possibilities.

You may also decide to let go of desires which no long interest you. Then you can focus on what's really important.

Integrity is essential for manifesting desires

Integrity can be defined as the state of being whole: our actions are aligned with what we say to ourselves and others.

Let's start with what we say to others. Most of us feel bad if we make a commitment and don't fulfil it – at least if someone points it out to us. (Some people have a habit of casually making promises and then forgetting about them.)

Lack of integrity leads to self-doubt. We question our ability to fulfil our commitments. We feel powerless. This makes it much harder to manifest our desires.

There are two solutions. The first is to do what we said we would. The second is to tell the person concerned that we aren't going to do it. We can explain why.

The other aspect of integrity is what we say to ourselves. When we tell ourselves we're going to do something and don't do it, maybe no one else hears about it, but it still eats away at our trust in ourselves.

The first time I visited my guru, Swamiji, in India, he asked us to make a list of our desires. One of mine was to travel in a particular country. He told me I should either do it or drop it – which puzzled me at the time. (I decided to drop it, which was a great relief.)

I realized afterwards that the idea of travelling in that country was a very old one. I was planning to go there when I was a student. A war broke out, so I didn't go. Now I realized that I no longer had much interest in travelling there. Letting go of that old, redundant desire felt good. It created space for something new to happen.

Integrity is synonymous with power and responsibility. We do what we say we will – with ourselves and others. When we radiate integrity, the cosmos responds accordingly.

SUMMARY

- You may have been complying with social norms for years. Now it's time to ask yourself what you really want.
- In order to identify your true desires, start by removing the other desires, which fall into four categories:

    1. Borrowed desires, when you want something because other people want it.
    2. Complicating desires, which lead to more complications instead of resolving an issue.
    3. Conflicting desires, when you have two opposing desires.
    4. Contradicting desires, when you wish for something, but your actions or intentions contradict that wish.

- Don't worry about how your desires are going to manifest – the Cosmic Intelligence will take care of that.
- Choose your words carefully. You're taking responsibility for the manifestation.
- It helps to see and touch what you're manifesting.
- Remember that your desires are likely to evolve.
- Once you're clear about your desire, stay focused.
- Integrity, when our actions are aligned with what we say to ourselves and others, is essential for manifesting our desires.

2

THINKING WILL ONLY GET YOU SO FAR

Let me start by explaining how I got into this subject. Like most people, I was brought up to see myself as a separate body/mind. I believed that if I worked hard I'd have a good life. On paper, I did everything right: I worked hard at school. Then I studied Economics at Cambridge and worked in banking and management consultancy, in London and Chicago. That was followed by an MBA at INSEAD in France, where I won first prize.

I knew I didn't want to go back to banking or consultancy – I was looking for a more balanced life. Fund management and recruitment both appealed to me as alternatives. A classmate helped me to get an interview with Europe's largest independent fund management firm, which offered me a job. I took a couple of months off over the summer and joined them in September.

Within a few days I felt very uneasy. First of all, I realized that the analytical skills I'd acquired were of limited use. My new colleagues were doing very well with basic techniques. Secondly, I noticed that the best fund managers were also highly intuitive. (By intuition, I mean 'immediate insight without reasoning', as the *Encarta World English Dictionary* defines it.) After years of studying analytical subjects and learning languages, my intuition seemed to have died. I considered moving into recruitment, but realized that it also required intuition. Then I felt stuck. I couldn't see a way out.

Within a short while I was waking up very early, losing sleep and spending the day plagued by chaotic, negative thoughts. I felt suicidal and went to see various doctors and psychiatrists. They all told me the same thing: 'You have clinical depression.'

The treatment included medication, which made me sleep for ten or more hours a day. Even when I was awake, I was mentally numb. My limbs felt heavy. I was unable to do my job properly and felt like a complete failure. Over a period of 16 months, I resigned or was fired from 3 jobs in succession.

Every now and then I'd think of a job that I hadn't already considered. Then the depression would recede for a while. I'd feel bright, energetic and optimistic. Then I'd gather some more information and conclude that job wasn't going to work either – at which point I'd sink back into depression.

My mum did her best to help. She was a physiotherapist, so we were no strangers to doctors or medication. We went for long walks – and talked and talked – but didn't find an answer.

In addition to the medication, I travelled several times a week to a big house in Islington, North London, for Freudian psychoanalysis. As you might expect, I lay on a couch while a man with a white beard asked me about my childhood. He analysed me for 18 months – on and off – but there was no solution beyond talking. I knew I had to keep searching for the answer to my problems.

It was becoming clear to me that I didn't want to live this way. I felt as though I'd taken a wrong turn. How come I was perfectly qualified for jobs I didn't want to do, and lacked the intuition required for the jobs I *did* want to do?

It was a living nightmare. While I was asleep I was fine. As soon as I woke up – often very early in the morning – the whole thing started again. I felt I was trying to fix something that was wrong with me, but I didn't know what it was or how to fix it.

The suffering continued to the point where suicide seemed like a logical solution. If my mind and body didn't exist, then maybe there wouldn't be any more suffering.

The suicidal thoughts weren't a complete surprise. I grew up in Leicester, in the centre of England, and attended Wyggeston Grammar School for Boys. There were no fees to pay, and many of the teachers were excellent. One year, 18 pupils won places at Oxford and Cambridge, which was high for a school in the state sector. But there were suicides among the Oxbridge crowd within a few years of leaving Wyggeston.

From my early twenties, I'd had the feeling that I might not live beyond the age of 27. The suffering was now acute. I was living in South Kensington, near the Queen's Tower at Imperial College, which is 87m (285ft) tall. One afternoon in January it occurred to me to climb the stairs and jump off the top. I wrestled with the door at the foot of the tower, but it was locked.

My parents persuaded me to go and stay with them in Wiltshire, where I met two more psychotherapists. The first was medically qualified. I sat in his office and he invited me to look out of the window. 'See all those people walking around out there?' he said, 'They aren't talking about killing themselves.' I peered at them and replied, 'No, I suppose not.' This wasn't helping me. I still felt completely stuck.

The second psychotherapist was a very relaxed, confident man with no medical qualifications – who'd also worked as a gardener. He looked at me and said, 'We have a saying in psychotherapy: never waste a good depression.'

This was the first big clue in my search for a solution. I'd tried as hard as I could to be successful and happy – in that order – by thinking a lot and taking action continuously. But I'd run into what seemed like a brick wall. Clearly I was missing something. It was time to find another way.

While I was growing up, my dad worked as a sales manager. He used to take me with him to business lunches, where I met his customers and the salespeople who reported to him.

The salespeople were generally far less academic than I was. They didn't have university degrees. They didn't seem inclined to kill themselves either. On the contrary, they seemed to be enjoying life. Looking back on my childhood, it occurred to me that I could now learn something from them.

We didn't learn about sales at business school and I realized I knew very little about it. I did understand that selling required intuition, which I didn't seem to possess anymore. Maybe this was the way forward – doing something I didn't understand but found intriguing. Looking back, this was the point when I realized that constant thinking wasn't getting me anywhere. I needed to go beyond thinking and find a new way to live.

For the next few years I worked in sales and marketing: in financial services, software and then environmental products. Throughout this period I was self-employed or running my own business. Soon I was working in Belgium, France and Germany, with people from all over the world.

I was still struggling financially, but at least I was getting to the heart of the matter, by observing people who were successful without thinking all the time.

Some of my colleagues were very successful, which I found mystifying. I was performing more or less the same actions, *without* achieving similar results. I knew I needed to change, but I couldn't figure out how. Of course there were clues. An American colleague told me I didn't love myself. That rang true but he didn't tell me *how* to love myself. Another told me to 'put my ego in the bank', which sounded sensible, but I didn't know how to do that either. If someone had told me I needed to run down the street in a Donald Duck outfit, I would have tried that. But there were no clear instructions – only concepts or anecdotes that seemed to contain a grain of truth.

At this point I realized that I couldn't work any harder in the outer world – I needed to work on myself. My colleagues were very keen on personal development, including motivational techniques and neuro-linguistic programming. I found some of it useful, but it didn't solve my underlying problem. With hindsight, I recognize that I still saw myself as a separate body/mind, trying to deal with lots of other body/minds. This was a lesson in itself. The sales people were all self-employed, so I couldn't control them. Despite my efforts to motivate and cajole them, the results were very poor. I wasn't earning enough to pay my bills, and was running out of money.

Eventually I got completely stuck, as I described in *The Power of Letting Go*. I was living in the 17th Arrondissement – a beautiful part of Paris. However, there were lots of strikes, including on the Metro. Commuters were driving their cars into the city, which was soon in gridlock. I was already living from my savings. Now our business ground to a halt. I ran out of money and couldn't pay the rent or the grocery bills. My relationship was coming to an end. I was borderline depressed and had sciatica, which made it very difficult to walk. In short, my life wasn't working out the way I wanted.

When I stood back from the situation, the contrast was stark. Ten out of ten for effort: I'd been working hard for years. Zero out of ten for results: I was broke and ill, trying to solve several problems at once by thinking and taking action continuously.

There was clearly something I hadn't understood – but what was it? If I could find out what I was doing wrong and change it, then surely my life would change too – like switching on a lightbulb in a dark room.

I now see my failures as a blessing. Life was showing me several things. First of all, thinking and working hard aren't enough for us to manifest our desires and fulfil our potential. Secondly, personal development wasn't the way forward. I'd been trying to improve myself, develop myself, or whatever you want to call it, but it wasn't working. Later I heard the phrase: 'The person you're trying to develop doesn't exist.' At the same time, I knew the solution to my problem was somewhere inside me.

Maybe my story resonates with you. Things aren't working, but you don't know what to do about it. Maybe you've begun your own search for answers to the problems you face. It doesn't have to be depression that makes you start looking. For some people it's bereavement, divorce, illness, an accident, losing a job, closing down a business, losing all your money, having your reputation destroyed or being forced to leave your home country.

I'd tried to think my way to a solution. I'd tried working all the time. I'd also tried personal development, in the hope of thinking and working more effectively. But all of this was getting me nowhere – hence the low-level feeling of depression. In my case, the situation was unsustainable, so I *had* to change. With hindsight, that was another blessing.

Many people carry on for years – even decades – without experiencing a major crisis. They just about hang onto their careers and relationships, while keeping their health problems under control. Life is painful, but not painful enough for them to do much about it. However, at some point we realize we *have* to change.

From individual effort to spiritual experience

My sales training was based on the same assumption as university and business school: that we're all separate body/minds trying to get what we want and avoid what we don't want. The same was true of what I'd been learning about personal development. Then I found a different approach.

Having attended church and Sunday school between the ages of five and fifteen, I felt there was some intelligence beyond my individual brain. Observing nature – including my own body – I could see there was something extremely clever going on. It seemed highly unlikely to me that life was a random occurrence.

I came across a novel called *A Rich Man's Secret*,[3] which sounded promising. The main character is told he should keep 'returning to now', so I decided to give that a go. I kept returning my attention to the present moment, and soon noticed that I was having fewer and fewer thoughts. The stress was beginning to drop away.

Perpetual mental and physical effort had been getting me nowhere, so I decided to stop. Since the Metro was on strike and the roads were gridlocked, I couldn't go very far anyway. Instead of working, I kept reading the novel and returning to the present moment. I found myself being present more and more.

I soon noticed that my intuition had become much stronger. The fewer thoughts I had, the clearer things became. I began to have a feeling about people I met – and situations in which I found myself – without the need for some elaborate thought process. Since my intuition seemed to have woken up again, I decided to take another look at recruitment, and executive search in particular.

I let go completely and asked to be guided to the right job or business. I also started buying British newspapers. A few days later an advertisement appeared in *The Sunday Times* for consultants to join one of the world's largest executive search firms, recruiting senior executives and board members.

I applied for the job. I also sent my CV to 26 other firms, and had interviews with some of them. The first firm made me an offer, which I accepted.

The base salary was 98 per cent of what I'd been trying and failing to earn for seven years. The bonus took me significantly beyond that. I later discovered I was a perfect fit with their list of criteria.

My ideal job landed in my lap. I moved smoothly from one country to another, and from one sector to another, to a job that fitted me perfectly. This was my first experience of consciously surrendering – by asking to be guided.

For the first time in my life, I had a job I could see myself doing for the long term. I enjoyed recruiting senior executives and board members, and seemed to be pretty good at it. It was well paid and still gave me enough time to read and attend courses on spirituality.

One of the books I read was *The Power of Now*,[4] by Eckhart Tolle, which gave me a better understanding of what I'd learned in Paris. I found that if I kept returning to the present moment, I could do my job well, without being affected too much by other people's mood swings. This new approach to life seemed to be working.

I achieved the revenue targets the firm had set, and was promoted to partner four years later. The following year, there was a big economic downturn and I was fired, along with many colleagues. As before, I let go completely and asked to be guided. I sat at home completing a project. Then the chief financial officer of a well-known public company contacted me. He was being promoted and invited me to recruit his replacement.

I had a set of business cards printed and took the train to the company's headquarters, where I met the CFO and the chief executive. We agreed terms and I got started. This assignment led to another, then another. You could say that I started my own business. In reality, I surrendered and asked to be guided – then a new business appeared. Soon I had three colleagues.

PURE CONSCIOUSNESS

Around the same time, an American friend recommended I learn Transcendental Meditation[5] – otherwise known as TM – at the Maharishi Foundation.

This gave me a daily experience of pure consciousness – the fundamental, unchanging reality that underlies all existence. It's the supreme state of awareness beyond mind, body and senses.

Solutions to problems and creative ideas started coming to me during meditation. I began to write books, which got published. Co-authors, publishers and my literary agent appeared at just the right time. TM even removed practically all of my jet lag.

However, I still felt stuck – again – in terms of both money and relationships. When I looked around at other meditators, many of them also seemed to be stuck. Some were consistently healthy but broke. Others had money but kept experiencing setbacks in their health or relationships – or both.

I didn't know how to stop being stuck. Since I couldn't solve this problem intellectually, I meditated and asked to be guided.

Then I let go completely. I surrendered. I became open to all possibilities and stopped trying to control how things happened in my life. In the meantime I carried on with my activities as normal.

A few days later I received a message from a lady I'd met a couple of times before. She invited me to an event in London on a Sunday afternoon in May. The invitation mentioned the phrase 'Living Advaita',[6] which immediately got me interested – it sounded like being in tune with the cosmos all the time. Maybe this was the solution I was looking for.

The event took place in a church which had been converted into a health club. There were lots of people wearing white Indian clothes, with red cotton scarves known as *kavis*. Many of them had *vibhuti* (white ash) on their foreheads, and *kumkum* (a dark red dot) between their eyes.

In a corner of the room was a screen with a very poor internet connection. On the screen was a man with brilliant white teeth, sitting on a golden throne. He was speaking in a strong South Indian accent, calmly and deliberately, with a big smile now and then. It was Swamiji.

Experiencing pure consciousness

Some people experience pure consciousness during silent meditation. It helps the mind become still and transcend the ordinary fluctuations of thoughts and emotions.

This isn't merely mental calmness. It's a direct perception of your own true nature as consciousness itself. You realize you aren't the body or the mind. You're the pure awareness that underlies all existence.

Get ready to experience the world differently

If you *insist* on using your *mind* all the time, you'll need to think *a lot*. This includes analysing everything that isn't working and thinking up solutions. Then you'll need to take action – or persuade other people to do so. Let's say you start a family, or get promoted at work, or start a business that grows. The more people and resources you deal with, the more stress you'll experience. There'll be more problems to analyse and solve. There'll be more situations requiring your intervention. You'll also find yourself taking lots and lots of action, much of which will be wasted. That sounds exhausting, doesn't it?

We experience the world differently as soon as we move on from the mind to Cosmic Intelligence. Instead of constantly thinking, we ask the intelligence that's running the cosmos to manifest through us and fulfil our desires. I'm going to show you how to do this consistently.

SUMMARY

- Pure consciousness is the supreme state of awareness beyond mind, body and senses.
- It's time to move on, from the mind to Cosmic Intelligence.
- Instead of constantly thinking, we ask the intelligence that's running the cosmos to manifest through us.

3

YOU'RE MANIFESTING ALL THE TIME

As I said in the introduction, most of us assume we're a body/mind trying to get what we want and avoid what we don't want. This assumption is rooted in the idea that we're *separate* from everyone and everything. The implication is that, if you want something to happen, you either take action yourself or you get someone else to do it. For example, if you're thirsty you go to the kitchen and get a glass of water. If you want something for your home, you either go and fetch it or you have it delivered.

Most of the time, simple tasks can be performed in accordance with classical physics, which dominated scientific thinking in the 18th and 19th centuries. If you apply a physical force to an object in a particular direction, the outcome is highly predictable.

I pursued this approach until my mid-twenties. The harder I worked, the better things turned out. There seemed to be a correlation between effort and results. However, at the age of 26 – when I left business school – I discovered that mental and physical effort was *not* enough for me to manifest all my desires. Maybe you've made a similar discovery.

During my search for a solution to my problems, I read several books about the 'law of attraction'. Simply put, it says that positive thoughts bring positive results into your life, while negative thoughts bring negative results. This sounded perfectly sensible, but I couldn't make it work for me. No matter how much positive thinking I did, I couldn't manifest everything I wanted in my life. Why not?

In the meantime I met lots of entrepreneurs. I noticed that some were much more successful than others. A few of them had launched a series of successful businesses. Others were 'one-hit wonders' who had one success which they failed to replicate. There were many others who failed over and over again. Why?

You may also be looking at your health, wealth and relationships – then scratching your head and saying, 'How come so many things are happening that I *don't* want?'

The answer is that we're manifesting all the time, but we do so unconsciously. To put it bluntly, we don't know what we're doing.

If I look back at the time when I was really struggling, I can see that I was only vaguely aware of my negative thoughts and emotions. I assumed that if I kept thinking and working hard, everything would turn out the way I wanted. It didn't.

Listen to yourself

Try this:

Throughout the day, listen carefully to what you say to yourself and to other people. When you have time, sit quietly on your own and write it all down.

What did you find?

Here are some common examples of what we say to ourselves and may even blurt out to other people.

- 'This is unfair.'
- 'Life is hard.'
- 'I'm such a loser.'
- 'S/he said I wouldn't be any good at this.'
- 'S/he's an idiot/narcissist/egomaniac/pain in the . . .'
- 'People are so stupid.'

- 'Why does nothing I do work out?'
- 'Where have all the good (wo)men gone?'
- 'I'll just keep trying. Maybe I'll succeed one day. There isn't much else I can do.'
- 'Let's give this one last try.'

All these statements and questions arise in your *inner space*. (The Sanskrit term is *chidakasha*, which can be translated as 'consciousness space'.) This is the feeling and awareness of yourself when you close your eyes and look inwards. You're manifesting from your inner space. Even though some of these examples are questions, they still have a massive effect on what happens in your life.

When we recognize that we're manifesting all the time, we experience life in a new way. I'm going to show you how to manifest from consciousness – instead of thinking a lot.

THE UNCLUTCHING TECHNIQUE

This will show you how to experience pure consciousness. In 2000 Swamiji introduced a technique called unclutching. Please do this:

- **Sit in a quiet place and close your eyes.**
- **Every time a thought appears, you have a choice:**

  You can engage with the thought – by thinking about it, resisting it or suppressing it.

Alternatively, you can choose *not* to engage with the thought. You simply distance yourself from it.

- **All you need to do is choose *not* to engage with each thought. Just stand back from it. Unclutch.**

  Most of us make an unconscious choice each time. We keep choosing to engage with our thoughts. When a thought arises, we choose to:

  - **Reflect on it**
  - **Mull it over**
  - **Resist it**
  - **Suppress it**
  - **Try to forget about it**
  - **Make a joke about it**

If we do any of these things, we're likely to have one thought after another. It's a chain reaction.

The unclutching technique liberates us from this drama. Unclutching boils down to this: when a thought arises, you don't engage with it. You simply distance yourself. You stand back from it. This is a vital step in moving on, from the mind to Cosmic Intelligence.

If you keep standing back from your thoughts, they'll lose their power over you. You'll notice that thoughts appear and disappear in consciousness. That consciousness is *you*.

Unclutching can feel lazy or scary at first

When I was learning to unclutch, it felt lazy. I was used to engaging with any thought that popped into my head. It took a while to get used to *not* engaging.

Many people find unclutching scary. We've been conditioned to believe that we need to think a lot and stay in control. We're afraid that if we unclutch – if we stop engaging with our thoughts – our lives will fall apart. In reality, the opposite happens. When we unclutch, everything falls into place.

The experience of unclutching – and allowing life to unfold naturally – shows us there's an intelligence running the cosmos, including our bodies and the world around us. If we tune into this intelligence, we experience bliss and fulfilment. We allow the intelligence that's running the cosmos to run our lives.

This isn't something that lends itself to testing in a laboratory – there are too many variables. I invite you to unclutch sincerely and see for yourself.

When we unclutch we engage fully with life

As newborn babies we're unclutched. We're naturally in a state of restful awareness. Then, from early childhood onwards we construct an *identity* which is based on our experiences, language, ethnicity, nationality, education, successes, failures, qualifications and aspirations.

At the same time, both fear and greed are instilled in us, by our parents, our teachers and others. We're rewarded if we do one thing. We're punished if we do some other thing. This continues once we leave education and start work.

In adulthood we're driven by fear and greed. We do lots of planning and goal-setting. We also try to manipulate others using fear and greed.

Many successful entrepreneurs readily admit they're motivated by fear. They may have left a war-torn country, or lost a parent, or suffered a debilitating childhood illness. Even billionaires suffer from fear.

Later in this book I'll show you how to remove the source of the fear. In the meantime, the unclutching technique will help you to start letting go of fear and greed – and declare powerful cognitions instead – as I'll explain in the next chapter.

If we unclutch we engage fully with life, while remaining detached from the outcome.

When I unclutch, I:

- **Am present, without making any effort.**
- **Enjoy the moment.**
- **Have insights without analysing.**
- **Remember things more easily.**
- **Accept the present moment, instead of resisting it.**
- **Take the right action at the right time.**
- **Find myself in the right place at the right time.**
- **Allow my desires to be fulfilled in the best possible way.**

We can unclutch all day long. If you're stressed or depressed, unclutching will give you an immediate break from negative thoughts. You can unclutch from any thought, including labels, judgements, expectations, comparisons, opinions and conclusions. When we unclutch, we allow thoughts to happen – and let go of them. We don't engage with them or give any meaning to them.

Your mind isn't a machine

The mind is often seen as some kind of machine that needs to be fixed now and then. Hence the term 'mental breakdown'. But what if we viewed it differently?

Swamiji describes the mind as an ocean in which fish are jumping, randomly and spontaneously. If you look at it this way, there's no need to start connecting thoughts and making meaning out of them. We can allow the fish to jump as much as they want. If they're distracting us, we can unclutch.

Of course, we do have underlying patterns that create problems in our lives. I'll show you how to identify and remove those in the next chapters. But any thoughts that need to happen will do so automatically. Your mind will become an instrument. It will no longer be your master.

When I left business school I felt as though my mind had taken over my life and become my master. I've met many other people who say they can't stop thinking. Unclutching liberates us from endless thoughts.

STRENGTHENING YOUR INTUITION

Earlier I defined intuition as 'immediate insight without reasoning'. There's no conscious thought process. We just have an insight or a feeling or a sudden understanding.

I'm going to describe three main explanations for these insights. In each case, unclutching will make your intuition stronger.

Explanation 1: Intuition comes from subconscious pattern recognition and prior experience

This is a common explanation in Western psychology which, as I mentioned, assumes that each of us is a separate body/mind.

If we unclutch, we stop having thoughts – if only for a few seconds. Then we can connect what we're seeing or hearing with a pattern in the data stored in our brains. We can use that pattern to form an opinion straight away.

For example, having worked in executive search for many years, I've met thousands of chief executives and chief financial officers. With that amount of data stored in my brain, it's not surprising that I notice patterns that differentiate the best candidates from the rest.

I can then check my intuition by gathering more information and doing further analysis. For example, in the case of interviews, I can gather more information about a candidate by talking to their former colleagues and looking at the financial performance of the companies they've managed.

Here's another example: when I lived in Paris I knew a teenager who seemed to have very strong intuition. I later discovered that he worked part-time in a Chinese restaurant. He had a feeling about whether a particular customer was going to leave a decent tip – and he was usually right. According to this first explanation, his feeling would be based on his previous experience.

Explanation 2: Intuition comes from evolution or instinct

Sometimes we don't have the luxury of pattern recognition or analysis. I once met a former US marine who had survived urban combat. He described rushing into buildings during battles in places he'd never been to before, and making the correct choices between turning left and turning right.

There are firefighters who make similar decisions when they enter a building that could collapse or be engulfed in flames at any moment. Their choice of direction can make the difference between life and death. There's very little data, and almost no time to make a decision. It's often argued that – in these situations – our intuition comes from unconscious processes in our brains inherited from our ancestors – which we might call *instinct*. They enable us to adapt to our environment and survive as a species.

If you need to make a decision urgently, with very little information, unclutching will help you. The stream of thoughts will die down and you'll be clear about what you need to do.

Explanation 3: Intuition comes from pure consciousness

There are situations in which we receive an insight or instruction out of the blue – without any data. In her book *You Do Know: Learning to Act on Intuition Instantly*,[7] Becky Walsh describes how intuition can give you a positive feeling to move away from danger. She tells me, 'In the country lanes of Somerset, I've found my foot coming off the accelerator and onto the brake long before seeing a car driving too fast for the corner, turning onto the wrong side of the road. The feeling isn't a negative "gut instinct", it's being in flow with what's around you.'

Intuition can also give you a positive feeling to move towards someone or something. For example, when I go to networking events, I don't introduce myself to everyone in the room. I stand still and unclutch. Sometimes I have a feeling I should speak to a particular person. Sometimes the right person comes and speaks to me. (I'll say more on this later when I talk about surrender.)

In these situations, intuition can arise from pure consciousness. The more you practise the techniques I'm describing in this book, the more you'll experience intuition from pure consciousness.

In the next chapter I'll show you how to find and remove the pain patterns that are running your life – and generating lots of negative thoughts. You can then unclutch from any thoughts that do appear in your inner space. This will help you to avoid 'false intuition', which is a projection of past conditioning.

If you stop engaging with the stream of thoughts, you'll experience an empty space. The *immediate insight without reasoning* will suddenly appear in that empty space. It comes out of the blue.

These days I often experience intuition from pure consciousness. This book will help you do the same.

The difference between unclutching and mindfulness

If you're familiar with mindfulness, you may be wondering how it differs from unclutching.

I learned mindfulness from a book initially. At its simplest, it works like this. First of all, you place your attention on your breath or on one of your senses – such as the weight of your body on the chair, or the air touching your skin. Every time your attention wanders, you bring it gently back to your breath or to one of your senses. If you keep doing this, you'll find you're present more and more throughout the day.

Unclutching is even simpler. When a thought arises, you choose NOT to engage with it. The mind 'clutches' automatically when thinking is required, but when you unclutch you step back from it.

Creativity occurs in pure consciousness

Please note that, when you unclutch, you're still going to move your body when necessary. I'm not talking about sitting in a cave doing nothing. It's a question of what *guides* your body to take action. Most people simply react to situations and think a lot.

It's often assumed that progress comes from thinking. However, many artists, musicians, scientists and business people have received brilliant ideas and solutions to problems when they *weren't* thinking.

I describe these experiences as *downloads.* The idea or solution appears when I'm *not* thinking. It comes out of the blue. This started happening regularly when I learned Transcendental Meditation.

An extreme example is Srinivasa Ramanujan,[8] regarded as one of the greatest mathematicians of all time, and played by Dev Patel in the movie *The Man Who Knew Infinity.* With very little training in pure mathematics, he compiled nearly 3,900 mathematical results – most of which have since been proven correct – before his death at the age of 32. He said at one point he had visions of scrolls of complex mathematics unfolding before his eyes.

As a more recent example, JK Rowling was sitting on a delayed train from Manchester to London when she suddenly had the idea of a boy wizard who went to wizarding school. She said that Harry Potter and Hogwarts came out of nowhere.

How about you?

Have you ever had an idea that appeared when you weren't thinking – and then materialized over the next few hours, days, months or years? It could be a book, a painting, a piece of music, a business, a product or a solution to a problem.

Please write down any examples that come to you now. (Others may appear when you aren't thinking.)

Now practise unclutching. You can sit and unclutch for as long as you want, using the instructions earlier in this chapter (see page 45). You can also unclutch over and over again during the day, as I do. You'll start to have a feeling about what's going on around you, and what you should do next.

When we unclutch, we go beyond the limitations of the mind. We experience the vast, unbound Cosmic Intelligence.

SUMMARY

- Mental and physical effort isn't enough for us to manifest all our desires.
- We're manifesting all the time from our inner space, but we do so unconsciously. That's why we often manifest what we don't want.
- The unclutching technique will give you the experience of pure consciousness. When a thought arises, you don't engage with it. You simply distance yourself.
- Unclutching can feel lazy or scary at first but when we unclutch, we engage fully with life.
- Your mind is like an ocean in which fish are jumping, randomly and spontaneously, so there's no need to start connecting thoughts.
- When we unclutch, our intuition becomes much stronger. Intuition is like a muscle we can strengthen through the practice of unclutching.
- There's a difference between unclutching and mindfulness.
- Creativity occurs in pure consciousness.

4

FIND THE PAIN PATTERNS THAT ARE RUNNING YOUR LIFE

As I said in the introduction, most of us struggle in at least one area of our lives – maybe two or three of them at once. We're creating our reality, but most of us do so *unconsciously*. That's why we frequently manifest what we don't want – while failing to manifest what we *do* want.

It all starts with our negative beliefs – or pain patterns – which grow like branches on a tree and start manifesting in our lives. Each painful incident adds another twig or branch to the tree. The tree also has a root pattern, which I'll explain shortly.

Your pain patterns are running your life, creating situations that you don't want. If you move to a country on the other side of the world, the same pain patterns will run your life. You can't escape from them. You've suppressed the pain, which is now stored in your body.

To manifest your desires, you *have* to remove the pain patterns

I've read lots of books about manifestation. Maybe you have too.

For most people, the results are patchy. You may have noticed that some things manifest easily in your life, while others don't. This is because our pain patterns prevent some things from manifesting but not others. If you look at other people, you'll see they're in a similar situation, with their own set of pain patterns. Different people struggle in different ways.

The good news is, there's a solution. Swamiji has provided a technique based on an ancient principle. He calls it the Science of Completion℠ which I explained in *The Power of Letting Go*. If you've read it, that's great. I'm now going to restate the completion technique and then show you how to use it to manifest your desires.

On the one hand, we have desires: things we want to happen. On the other hand, we have *pain patterns* from the past which are stored in our bodies. These pain patterns have two effects:

- **First, we *don't* manifest some of our desires**
- **Second, we often manifest things we *don't* want**

The net result is that we manifest one undesired situation after another. Here are some examples of these pain patterns. They're conclusions about ourselves, other people, the world and life in general.

- **'I'm a failure'**
- **'I'm not good enough'**
- **'I can't trust people'**
- **'I can't have what I want'**
- **'Life is hard'**
- **'It isn't fair'**

Please note:

- ***You* came to each conclusion in response to an event in the past. *You* created each pain pattern that's running your life.**
- **You're still giving life to these pain patterns through your will and belief.**
- **You don't have to live with the same patterns for the rest of your life.**

To use another analogy, pain patterns are like faulty software on a computer. You need to delete the bugs – then rewrite your software and manifest your desires.

Feel the pain

Let me ask you a question:

What's the earliest painful incident you can remember?

- Close your eyes and become that age again.
- Take a pen and a piece of paper. Write down what's happening and how you feel about it.

The pain is real

We all have pain patterns, which we can trace back to our early childhood, between the ages of two and seven. It could be something as serious as child abuse or as small as being told you can't have an ice cream.

Some of us say, 'Everything's fine. I had a great childhood – all things considered.' This is just a way of suppressing the pain. It continues to run your life.

From the age of two onwards, we develop a vocabulary, which enables us to come to conclusions about ourselves, other people, the world and life in general. These conclusions are stored in our bodies in the form of pain patterns. In the meantime, we've suppressed the painful memory and may even have forgotten about it.

I certainly wasn't aware of the pain patterns stored in my body. All I knew was that my life wasn't working the way I wanted. The completion technique heals our pain patterns. It makes us whole. It makes us complete.

THE COMPLETION TECHNIQUE

- Swamiji defines **incompletions** as 'incidents, memories, wrong cognitions from the past that are occupying the present and affecting our future.' An incompletion is a painful incident which you haven't completed. You haven't lived it fully from beginning to end, so it's still stored in your body.
- Swamiji defines **completion** as 'looking at the past with a new cognition. It's the absence of compulsive thought currents and behavioural patterns. Anything that increases your power is a truth.' I'm going to show you how to find the painful incidents in your past and complete them. You'll need the following:

1. A pen and a pad of paper.
2. A hand-held mirror in which you can see the whole of your face.
3. A quiet space where you won't be disturbed. (Otherwise, I recommend earplugs.)
4. A comfortable chair to sit in.

The completion technique[9] boils down to one simple instruction: re-live to relieve. (Note that, if the exercises in this book bring up past experiences that are too painful to deal with on your own, then do seek professional support, from either your doctor or a professional therapist.)

Re-live to relieve

This is completion, step by step:

1. The first and most important step is to *decide* that you're going to let go of the pain patterns that are holding you back.

2. Make a list of the incidents that have caused you pain in the past. These incidents could have occurred in any area of your life at any time from early childhood onwards.

3. Choose one incident.

4. Become that age again. Write down what you can see, hear and smell. What's happening? What are people saying? How do you feel about the situation? What do you conclude about yourself, other people, the world and life in general? Please write it all down, in the present tense and the first person (for example, 'I'm at home with my parents when . . .').

5. Now close your eyes and become that age again. Re-live the incident intensely from beginning to end, at least five times.

6. Now look at your face in the mirror. Connect with yourself by looking into your eyes. Become that age again. Re-live the incident – at least five times – by talking aloud to the person in the mirror.

Complete each incident over a period of 20 minutes.

Tips for successful completion

- Once you see your conclusions – or beliefs – on paper, you'll start to realize why things keep turning out the way they do. These are the beliefs that are manifesting in your life.
- Some people have difficulty identifying painful incidents between the ages of two and seven, so pick the earliest painful incident you can recall and re-live it intensely, even if it's later than the age of seven. Once you've re-lived that one, an earlier incident is likely to come to you. Please re-live that one too – at least five times with your eyes closed and at least five times talking to yourself in the mirror.
- You don't *recall* the incident – you *re-live* it. Become that age again, as though you're in a movie. If something painful happened when you were five years old, become five years old again, with the way you saw things at that age – not the way you see things now. The aim is to experience everything as a five-year-old.
- Allow any emotions to come up. If they do, *feel* them. There's no need to force anything.
- Don't try to *reconcile* yourself to what happened. For example, you might say it was understandable under the circumstances – or must have happened to plenty of other people. What matters is that something happened and *you* came to a conclusion which has been running your life ever since.
- The incident you need to complete may not be the obvious one. For example, my dad had multiple sclerosis and died of pneumonia. I was the first person on the scene – my mum was asleep and I was in a neighbouring room on a Sunday afternoon. I heard him stop breathing and went into the bedroom where he was

lying motionless. I woke my mum, then told the rest of the family. When I learned completion I understood that this episode hadn't had much effect on me. I realized that what really got me was an incident a few weeks later, watching my mum crying while buying flowers for the cemetery.

- **Don't dismiss any event as too minor. Maybe your parents refused to give you an ice cream, but you then concluded that 'life doesn't give me what I want'. Conclusions such as this can have an enormous impact on your life – for decades.**
- **Your mind may wander and you may lose track of how many times you've re-lived a particular incident. Solve this by counting on the fingers of one hand.**
- **Persistence is essential. Your mind will make every effort to distract you from the completion process.**
- **We simply re-live the experience intensely from beginning to end. Re-living allows the pain to leave the body. Some people feel more relaxed – or physically lighter – when this happens.**
- **When we're complete, we experience our natural state of blissful awareness.**

What not to do

Completing a painful incident can take several sessions. It's worth it. The more we re-live, the less power the painful incident has over us. Eventually, it becomes an empty memory with no emotional charge. I sometimes feel the change in my body when this happens. The tension or agitation falls away.

The challenge for most people is this: they don't follow the instructions! I'm *not* asking you to do any of the following:

- **Remember all aspects of that period of your life.**
- **Analyse the situation.**
- **Analyse yourself.**
- **Reconcile yourself to what happened.**
- **Accept that the way other people behaved was reasonable under the circumstances.**
- **Imagine what might have happened if things had been different.**
- **Re-imagine the incident in some way to make the memory less painful.**

The instruction is *re-live to relieve.* That's all. The end result of this process is that you'll see the past as it is – without any editing, interpretation or manipulation. You'll let go of the beliefs that have been holding you back. Then you'll be able to move on and manifest your desires.

The second time I visited Swamiji in India, I told him I'd practised completion every day for several weeks, to the point where my mind became almost silent for 24 hours. He grinned and gave me a thumbs-up with both hands. I knew I was on the right track.

Move on from pain

Follow these two steps to ensure that the pain is fully resolved and doesn't linger in your consciousness.

1. First make sure you've completed with the pain. Then you won't be re-creating the pain by focusing on it.

2. Only when you've completed with the pain, unclutch from it.

Completion works beautifully with unclutching

I've met many people who say they find it difficult to be present. Their minds keep wandering, with lots of thoughts about the past and the future. They usually find it hard to practise techniques such as mindfulness.

If you practise completion regularly, you'll steadily remove your pain patterns, so you'll have fewer thoughts – particularly negative ones. You can then unclutch from any thoughts that do appear in your inner space. You'll naturally be in the present moment. Ultimately, we understand that only the present moment exists. We can absorb information through our senses without imposing any patterns on them.

THE FIVE OR SIX PAIN PATTERNS THAT ARE RUNNING YOUR LIFE

Remember that pain patterns can create unwanted situations in any area of your life. One way to find them is to look at where you're stuck.

A few years ago I was short of money. When I looked back, my earliest memory of lacking money was at the age of 27 – when I left London to live with my parents in Wiltshire. I co-founded a software company and had very little income. For the first time in my life, I was short of money.

A wise friend told me that my pain pattern *wasn't* about money. (We often think that money is the problem because it's easy to measure.) She said it was something deeper that was *manifesting* as lack of money. I knew I needed to go further back – before the age of seven, which is when our pain patterns take root. At first

I was baffled. I was born in June and moved from infant school to junior school at the age of seven, so the incident I was looking for must have occurred at infant school or earlier. A few hours later, the incident I was looking for suddenly came to me.

I was around six years old when an optometrist came to our school to check our eyesight. After a few minutes, he announced that I was colour blind, so I couldn't join the armed forces or fly aeroplanes. I was very upset about that, since I loved aeroplanes. I felt I was being denied something. I also felt powerless to change the situation.

Many years later, I had no particular interest in flying aeroplanes, but it was clear that the six-year-old me had drawn four conclusions from failing the colour blindness test.

1. **'I'm a failure'**
2. **'It's impossible (for me to fly aeroplanes)'**
3. **'Life doesn't give me what I want'**
4. **'It isn't fair'**

I knew that *I* had come to these conclusions and that *I* could now remove them if I wanted to – using the completion technique. I switched off my computer and my mobile phone. Then I sat in an armchair and wrote down what had happened – in the first person and the present tense. I closed my eyes and re-lived the incident from beginning to end, over and over again:

> *I'm six years old. I'm at my school in Leicester. One day a man comes to test our eyesight. He takes out a big, white book. On each page is a large circle made up of lots of coloured dots. He asks me to tell him the number or letter that's hidden in the circle. I get a few of them right, but I can't see some of them.*

At the end he says, 'You're partially red-green colour blind. That means you can't join the army or the navy – or fly aeroplanes.' I leave the room feeling very upset. I love aeroplanes. When I meet my mum at the school gate I'm crying. I tell her what's happened. 'Oh dear,' she says, not sounding upset at all. 'Your cousin's the same.'

So it turned out that the pain pattern wasn't about money. Lack of money was a *manifestation* of my beliefs or conclusions, which were 'I'm a failure', 'It's impossible', 'Life doesn't give me what I want', 'It isn't fair'. In this case, I concluded that it was impossible for me to fly aeroplanes. My belief in impossibility then stayed with me for decades and showed up in many other areas of my life.

Notice what triggers you in daily life

Here are some ways of finding your pain patterns:

- **Notice how you're triggered by other people's posts and comments on social media.**
- **What about your reactions to politicians, celebrities and people in the news?**
- **How do you react to the people around you, at work, at home and in your social life?**
- **What about other people's behaviour on your journeys by car or public transport?**
- **Notice what comes up in your inner space when something doesn't work out the way you expected.**

Although it may not feel like it, all of these situations are blessings. Life is showing you your pain patterns and the incidents you need to complete.

Once you complete the original incident – and remove the pain pattern – your life will change for the better.

Ask yourself powerful questions

When we're struggling, many of us ask questions such as:

- **Why is this happening to me?**
- **What have I done to deserve this?**
- **How did I end up in this situation?**

Your mind is likely to respond with stories about how you did something wrong, how you took a wrong turn, how you should have done something different. It may even start telling you that this is a punishment for something you've done or failed to do. Questions like this make us feel powerless.

Please don't listen to your mind. Unclutch from all these thoughts. Again, life is showing you your pain patterns so you can complete with them by intensely re-living the original incident(s). As you let go of your pain patterns you'll feel better and better – and manifest your desires more and more easily.

Here are some powerful questions to ask yourself:

1. **What is life showing me?**
2. **Which of my pain patterns attracted this situation?**
3. **What are the pain patterns that keep manifesting in my life?**
4. **What are the incidents I need to re-live intensely in order to relieve them?**

The same kinds of people and situations will keep showing up in your life – until you complete with the pain pattern in question. Then life will stop showing you.

Listen to yourself

In order to find our incompletions – or pain patterns – we need to listen to ourselves. You can do this by sitting alone in silence and noticing what comes up. Please keep a pen and paper with you. Write down everything that's bothering you – all the painful thoughts and memories. Then complete each painful incident one at a time. I do this in several sessions if necessary. I keep coming back to my list until it's done.

1. Take a pen and paper, and look inwards.

2. Make a note of any person, situation or feeling that's bothering you.

3. Write down how you feel.

4. Ask yourself, 'What's my earliest memory of feeling this way?' What was the incident? Write it down in the present tense and the first person.

5. At the earliest opportunity, complete the incident by becoming that age again. See the incident the way you saw it at that age. Re-live the incident intensely to relieve it – at least five times with your eyes closed, and at least five times talking to yourself in the mirror.

Swamiji says the decision to complete is 80 per cent of what's required. If you *decide* you're going to complete, it begins to happen. If you write down the painful incidents as well as the conclusions you came to at that time, you'll start to see the pain patterns that are running your life now. They're connected in so many ways.

You may have pain patterns related to religion

Perhaps you shy away from anything spiritual. This is understandable, since human beings have frequently distorted spiritual teachings in order to control, suppress, or even torture people. There have also been religious leaders who've abused their followers. Completion will remove these pain patterns from your system. Then you can manifest your desires.

Pull your pain patterns out by the roots

We need to understand what's causing our suffering – and preventing our desires from manifesting. As I mentioned earlier, incompletions – or pain patterns – grow like a tree with roots. One painful incident can give rise to more than one pattern. Five or six pain patterns might be running your life and two or more of these may combine to form a root pattern. This is the fundamental pattern that creates a feeling of powerlessness. You feel stuck and unable to move forwards. As you complete the earliest painful incidents in your past – by re-living them intensely – a root pattern will emerge. (You may have more than one root pattern.)

COMPLETION LEADS TO MANIFESTATION

For years I was afraid of cycling in London, but that changed during the Covid pandemic. There was far less traffic, the air was cleaner, and cycle lanes were appearing all over the place. More and more people were cycling.

I wanted to buy a Brompton folding bicycle, but they quickly sold out. I called Brompton's headquarters and was told their stores wouldn't have any for another six months. No other retailer had any Bromptons either, except for the electric versions, which I didn't want. They also said I'd have to wait six months, at least. Some people were selling their Bromptons second-hand, but they were more expensive than the new ones, because you could get them right away. I didn't want to buy second-hand in case there was a fault or mechanical problem. I concluded that I would probably have to wait six months.

In the meantime, I discovered the pain patterns I described earlier. I also re-lived the episode with the colour-blindness test over and over again, intensely.

I then browsed various websites and thought about which Brompton I would like in an ideal world. There were many different models and colours. They were available with two, three or six gears. You could also choose between three types of handlebar. After a while I decided that my ideal bike would be an M3L in bright orange – one of over a hundred permutations. It felt like a pleasant fantasy. (Please note that I didn't write or type anything about this anywhere.)

I carried on re-living the episode with the colour-blindness test, intensely. I felt all the emotions. It became less painful each time.

A few days later I looked on the website of an independent retailer. Everything in the Brompton section was marked 'out of stock', *except* for an M3L in bright orange. At first I couldn't believe it. I looked again the next day. It was still there, so I ordered it, and it arrived.

This was one of my earliest experiences of completion leading to manifestation. When we're complete:

- **There are no internal conflicts or contradictions.**
- **Desires manifest, often in unexpected ways.**

The completion technique removes worry, fear and greed from our inner space. Then we automatically attract the best things.

When we're aligned with the Cosmic Intelligence, we manifest our true desires

You could of course dismiss the episode with the folding bicycle as a coincidence. I would agree it was a coincidence. Two events coincided: they happened at the same time. However, a coincidence isn't necessarily random. The Vedic tradition – among others – says there's an underlying intelligence which is manifesting everything all the time. You and I are part of it. My experience is that, when I'm aligned with that intelligence, I frequently experience helpful coincidences. Completion aligns us with the Cosmic Intelligence.

This episode illustrates another important point: manifestation isn't linear. In this case I was completing because I didn't have as much money as I wanted. In the process I manifested a folding bicycle. Similarly, some people do yoga and experience a breakthrough in their wealth. (I'll explain how to manifest wealth later in this book.) Our patterns in all three dimensions – health, wealth and relationships – are interconnected. When you complete a painful incident in one area of your life, you may see the results in another.

You'll know you've completed when your reality changes. When you complete, there's a shift in the world around you, which can include your body, other people and the situations in which you find yourself. In this case, the folding bicycle I wanted suddenly appeared when I intensely re-lived the colour blindness test, completing with the beliefs or patterns that were preventing me from manifesting my desires.

Here are the pain patterns I was holding on to. Consider your own as you read these examples:

- **'It's impossible'**

  Many people have this belief. Maybe it sounds familiar to you. In my case it seems to have started with 'It's impossible for me to fly aeroplanes'. After that, it popped up in many areas of my life – without my being aware of what was going on. It was also reflected in the world around me. When I lived in Paris, I frequently heard people say, *C'est pas possible* – 'It isn't possible.'

  When we complete with a negative thought pattern we can then declare a powerful cognition. In this case it could be, 'Everything is possible.' If you cognize that everything is possible, you may notice that things are manifesting in unexpected ways – beyond your logic.

  These days, my working assumption is that everything is possible. I become clear about *what* I'm manifesting, without worrying about *how* it's going to happen. The Cosmic Intelligence takes care of the how.
- **'I'm a failure'**

  You may also have this pattern. You're trying to succeed at something, while deeply convinced that you're a failure. No wonder you're frustrated! How can you expect to manifest your desires if you constantly have thoughts that undermine you? Completion is the solution.

Our incompletions are often triggered by contact with other people. Reunions are a good example. I once attended a dinner for alumni at St John's College, Cambridge. I met a friend in the bar afterwards and asked him how he was. He said he felt like a failure because he'd just been sitting between the chairman of one large, well-known company and the chief executive of another.

How about you?

Do you ever feel depressed or powerless when you attend reunions, networking events or conferences? Maybe it's enough just to think about talking to people with whom you compare yourself. Every time you're triggered, it's an opportunity to find your pain patterns and complete with them by re-living the original incidents intensely.

For years I was triggered when I met rich and successful people, until I completed with my pattern of 'I'm a failure' – starting with the colour-blindness test at the age of six. These days I can chat with self-made billionaires without feeling triggered.

If you keep looking inwards, you'll find other painful incidents that reflect your original conclusion: 'I'm a failure.'

During one completion session I remembered playing rugby at school. Someone passed me the ball and I kicked it instead of running with it. The opposing team then grabbed the ball. My teammates were disappointed in me. I felt like a failure. I felt much better once I'd re-lived this episode thoroughly in order to relieve it.

- **'It isn't fair'**

  Being told I couldn't fly aeroplanes felt deeply unfair to me. During one of my completion sessions, an experience around the age of ten flashed into my consciousness, so I re-lived it intensely.

I'm at junior school during a physical education class in the summer term. Our whole class is playing rounders (which is like baseball except the bat is much smaller and you hold it in one hand). I'm lining up behind the rest of my team who are waiting to bat. The boys in my team get bored and start a 'pile-up'. One jumps on top of the other until there's a whole pile of children on the ground. I'm standing at the back, watching what's going on.

In the meantime the game grinds to a halt. The other team, who are fielding the ball, stop and watch the pile-up. Our teacher is furious. He tells our team to stand in line. Then he takes his shoe and beats each of us over the backside, one by one. I protest that I wasn't involved, but it makes no difference. He beats me over the backside and it hurts like hell. I feel really upset about it and complain to my parents when I get home. It just isn't fair.

I re-lived this episode intensely – in several sessions.

- **'I'm unacceptable'**
  While I'm re-living, I remember my first day at school, so I re-live that as well:

I'm five years old and it's my first day at infant school. I want to make friends with the other children, so I start talking to them, but all they do is laugh at my accent. I want to join in, but they reject me.

I feel a dull ache in the centre of my chest. I hear the other children laughing at me. One of them calls me a 'bloody nootter'. They and the teacher are speaking in Leicester accents. I speak with a southern accent, like my parents. I don't make any new friends on my first day at school. I feel very bad about myself. I feel like an outsider – unacceptable.

The barber's chair

A day or two later I saw a post on social media by a friend who was saying that her six-year-old son didn't want to have his hair cut. I suddenly remembered a similar episode in my own childhood.

Before we moved to Leicester we lived in Hertford, just north of London. I remember celebrating my fourth birthday near Leicester, so I must have been around three years old when we lived in Hertford. I decided to re-live this earlier episode:

> *I'm in the barber's chair, feeling powerless. The barber is trying to cut my hair, which I don't want. I scream and scream, waving my arms and legs in frustration, and slide down into the chair. Eventually the barber cuts himself by accident.*

I re-lived this incident intensely, one morning after another. As before, the dull ache in the centre of my chest – and the tension throughout my body – gradually died down.

While I was doing all this completion, a doctor contacted me on LinkedIn. She hadn't read any of my books, it was simply a connection suggested by the algorithm. She and I met for lunch and became good friends. Coincidentally, she lived in Hertford, which I hadn't visited since I was three years old.

One day she invited me for lunch at her apartment. She met me at the train station and we walked to her apartment building. When we arrived I laughed. It was across the street from the house where I'd lived when I was three years old. After lunch we went for a walk and I took a photo of my old house. During one of my subsequent completion sessions, the image of the house in Hertford kept flashing in front of my eyes.

You could say it was a coincidence that I saw the house where I lived at the age of three while I was re-living the episode at the barber's. Again, I would agree it was a coincidence – and point out that coincidences aren't necessarily random. Life keeps showing us our pain patterns until we complete with them. Seeing and photographing the house helped me to become that age again and re-live the episode as a three-year-old.

The more we examine our pain patterns and complete with them, the clearer they become. In this case it started off as 'Life doesn't give me what I want'. That sounded a bit philosophical for a three-year-old. As I kept re-living, it became 'I'm not getting what I want'.

Here's a summary of what I discovered. Obviously, your patterns are likely to be different:

Incident	Age	Conclusions/pain patterns running my life ever since				
In the barber's chair, being forced to have my hair cut	3	'Life doesn't give me what I want'				
Children laughing at my accent on my first day at school	5	'Life doesn't give me what I want'	'I'm unacceptable'	'It isn't fair'		
Failing the colour-blindness test, which meant I couldn't fly planes	6	'Life doesn't give me what I want'	'I'm unacceptable'	'It isn't fair'	'I'm a failure'	'It's impossible'

The chart above shows how our pain patterns start, like branches on a tree. In this book I'm showing you how to uproot your pain-pattern tree. Imagine it's now lying on the ground in front of you. (Remember this image – I'll come back to it later.)

The pattern of 'I'm a failure' had clearly been preventing me from manifesting what I wanted. The cosmos was saying *tathastu*: so be it. Hey presto – I was a failure. Likewise, patterns such as 'I'm not getting what I want' and 'It's impossible' were preventing my desires from manifesting.

What about you?

I invite you to create your own chart to find the five or six pain patterns that are running your life.

Your 'achievements' are rooted in incompletion

Since most of us are brought up to see ourselves as separate body/minds, we often label desired outcomes as 'achievements'. If we look at them closely, we'll see that most or all of them are rooted in incompletion.

Here's a personal example. As I mentioned earlier, on my first day at school I concluded that I was unacceptable. It became one of the patterns running my life. I enjoyed playing soccer but wasn't particularly good at it, so I wasn't invited to join the team. However, I did discover a few activities that gained the approval of the people around me. They included mathematics, writing poetry and learning languages. Later on I became interested in economics and finance.

Between the ages of 16 and 18 I worked very hard at economics and languages, and took the Cambridge entrance examination. For the next three years I studied economics at St John's College. I also started teaching myself Spanish and planning a trip to South America, which is how I met my first girlfriend. Cambridge led to banking and plenty of money, followed by management consultancy and first prize at business school. Then I became suicidally depressed.

Looking back, I can see that my apparently successful life – until the age of 25 – was deeply rooted in incompletion. The conclusion that I was unacceptable was a big factor.

Here are a couple more examples:

- **A small child has a painful experience and concludes that s/he isn't safe, or the world is dangerous. It could be a childhood illness, or losing a parent, a family business going bankrupt, or growing up in a violent country where their life is in danger. For several decades they work extremely hard to accumulate wealth, hoping it will make them feel safe. However, the deep feeling of insecurity never leaves them. The pain pattern is still stored in their body.**
- **A child has a painful experience and comes to a conclusion about love. It could be 'I'm not loved', or 'Nobody cares about me'. They may go on to have a big family, but still find themselves looking for love.**

I enjoy reading or listening to interviews with people who are successful in their particular fields. Some of their pain patterns become obvious. Here are a couple of examples:

- **Someone who works hard to become famous, hoping it will give meaning to their life.**
- **A politician who tries to 'put things right' – and harms millions of people in the process.**

How about you? Which pain patterns have been driving you in your career, relationships and desire for success? To be clear, I'm not saying achievements are bad. I'm saying we don't need to suffer. In this book I'm showing you how to remove your pain patterns, so you can celebrate life and do amazing things.

SUMMARY

- Your pain patterns are running your life, creating situations that you don't want. If you want to manifest your desires, you have to remove the pain patterns.
- The completion technique heals our pain patterns. It makes us whole. It makes us complete.
- Incompletions are incidents, memories or wrong cognitions from the past that are occupying the present and affecting our future.
- Completion is looking at the past with a new cognition. It's the absence of compulsive thought currents and behavioural patterns.
- The completion technique boils down to one simple instruction: re-live to relieve. Completing a painful incident can take several sessions. It's worth it. You'll let go of the beliefs or cognitions that have been holding you back. Then you'll be able to move on and manifest your desires.
- Completion works beautifully with unclutching.
- Five or six pain patterns are running your life. You may have pain patterns related to religion.
- It's time to pull your pain patterns out by the roots. Completion leads to the manifestation of our desires.

- When we're aligned with the Cosmic Intelligence, we manifest our true desires. You'll know you've completed when your reality changes.
- Your 'achievements' are very likely to be rooted in incompletion.

5

STOP THOSE PAIN PATTERNS FROM RUINING YOUR LIFE

Imagine you're looking at a screen. You're about to watch a movie which contains your pain patterns about yourself, other people, the world and life in general. Now you start playing the movie. All kinds of things that you don't want to happen start appearing on the screen. You feel more and more frustrated and distressed.

Some people try to solve the problem by taking more and more action, which is like playing the movie faster and faster. Others start shouting at the screen.

The solution is obvious: change the movie! Remove your pain patterns before you start taking lots of action. That's what this chapter is about. We're going to focus on removing our pain patterns so we can manifest our desires. I'm also going to talk about *powerful cognitions*. These are specific, conscious beliefs that can transform your life.

Complete with your pain patterns to succeed in all areas of your life

In this book, I'm showing you how to succeed in your health, wealth and relationships – and anything else you want to manifest. But the first step is to address your pain patterns.

Earlier I described the five patterns that were running my life:

- **'Life doesn't give me what I want'**
- **'I'm unacceptable'**
- **'It isn't fair'**
- **'I'm a failure'**
- **'It's impossible'**

How about you?

Which pain patterns have you identified so far? Can you see how they're running your life? They may begin like this:

- 'I am . . .'
- 'People are . . .'
- 'The world is . . .'
- 'Life is . . .'
- 'God is . . .'

How to get rid of those pain patterns

Here are four personal examples:

1. Sciatica When I was living in Paris I suddenly experienced pain shooting down the inside of my right leg. It made walking very difficult. Sometimes it went away and I was able to run. Weirdly, the pain in my right leg sometimes disappeared and reappeared in my left leg. I have zero medical training, but it seemed to have something to do with my nerves. Since my dad had multiple sclerosis, I found this frightening.

A British friend who was a dentist came to stay. He said it was probably sciatica and asked me to stand up. Then he said the way I was standing was causing the problem. My posture in my lower back was irritating the sciatic nerve, sending pain shooting down my leg.

As I mentioned, my mum was a physiotherapist. On my next visit to the UK, she showed me some exotic-sounding exercises called 'pelvic tilting'. She also told me to avoid squashy chairs and car seats that could put my lower back in the wrong position. Within a few days, I felt much better. I haven't had sciatica for years.

I was still curious to know how I'd manifested sciatica in the first place, so I kept asking why. After learning the completion technique, I looked inwards.

I used to stand super-straight, like a soldier on parade. This made my backside stick out and led to sciatica. Why did I stand like that? I realized it went back to my early teens. My voice didn't break until I was 15½. Between the ages of 13 and 16, I was shorter than most of my classmates. My younger brother also grew taller than me. He soon became as tall as our dad. So I tried to make myself as tall as possible, by standing in this particular way.

Why was being tall important? When I looked inwards I realized it was because I felt unacceptable being shorter than other people. That took me straight back to my first day at school in Leicester, when my new classmates laughed at my accent and I felt unacceptable.

Now I can see the connection between my pain patterns and sciatica. Feeling unacceptable led me to stand in a particular way – which led to sciatica.

How about you? If you have physical pain in your body, I invite you to look inwards and ask why again and again. If you discover a pain pattern which is causing ill health, you can use the completion technique to remove it.

2. Relationships At one point it seemed as though I was surrounded by women in every area of my life, telling me what to do. There was clearly something I needed to complete in relation to women.

As usual, I took a pen and a pad of paper, and made a list of the incidents in my life that seemed to be connected, going back as far as I could. My earliest memory of feeling powerless in front of a woman was probably in the barber's shop in Hertford, when I was three years old. My dad was usually at work, so it was most likely my mum who put me in the barber's chair. Maybe that was when this pattern started.

I also remembered an incident when my mum was very angry. She said she'd pull my pants down and smack my bottom. Then she went ahead. It must have been well before my seventh birthday. While I was re-living this incident, I heard some conclusions: 'This is unfair. She's stopping me from doing what I want.'

Then I could see my powerlessness in romantic relationships. I'd treated two previous girlfriends like my boss. It was clear I'd been manifesting these situations for years. I kept re-living the painful incidents to relieve them. Eventually, the subtle charge left my body. Now it's just an empty memory.

In terms of what I like to call my 'pain-pattern tree', there seemed to be several pain patterns sprouting from 'Life doesn't give me what I want', which started at the age of three. They included:

- **'People are stopping me from doing what I want'**
- **'People keep telling me what to do'**

When I wrote down all the examples of these two beliefs manifesting in my life, I realized that most – but not all – involved women. There were also examples of men telling me what to do, which I found annoying, particularly when I felt they were misguided. I've carried on completing in this area. These days, if someone tells me what to do, I usually laugh.

I can trace the experiences of people telling me what to do – and stopping me from doing what I want – back to the much older conclusion that life doesn't give me what I want.

3. Divorce Late one evening I was sitting with a pen and a pad of paper, listening for any thoughts that might appear in my inner space. Something came up about divorce. I made a list of all the people I knew who'd been through at least one divorce. It was a long list. Then I carried on listening.

I realized I'd been afraid of divorce since I was around five years old. I was probably the only child in my class with divorced grandparents. On the one hand it was great, because my grandfather and grandmother had remarried and lived in different seaside towns, which meant holidays on different beaches. On the other hand I felt ashamed.

A memory came up and I re-lived it intensely:

> *My grandfather's second wife has died and he's moved to Leicester to be near us. He's living alone in an apartment a couple of miles away. I'm home from university for the Christmas holidays. My grandmother – his ex-wife – is staying with us over Christmas. My parents insist that neither grandparent must know the other is in Leicester, so neither gets upset. We open our Christmas presents in front of our grandmother. Then we tell her we're going to visit 'Mr Rotheray' – the code name for our grandfather. We re-wrap our presents, drive to his apartment and unwrap them again in front of him. The whole thing feels ridiculous.*

Re-living with my eyes closed wasn't painful at first. Then I realized that what bugged me was lying to my grandmother.

I become 19 years old, standing in the living room in Leicester. I'm putting on my dark blue coat, saying to her, 'We're going to see Mr Rotheray.' I feel amused but also guilty and ashamed.

What are your pain patterns?

I've just given you three examples of pain patterns that have appeared in different guises in various areas of my life and have described how I relieved them. How about you? Please write them down now – with a pen. Then you can re-live them to relieve them.

4. Wealth Some people associate spirituality with poverty, which is a misunderstanding. Money and other forms of wealth are useful commodities – that's all. It's the *attachment* to wealth through fear and greed that holds us back. For example, we cling to money for fear of losing it, hoping in vain that money will make us feel secure.

I knew this was an issue for me. There'd been times in my life when I was short of money, as well as times when money was abundant. The fact that I kept thinking about money was a sure sign that I was incomplete about it. It was disturbing my inner space.

I decided to complete with my patterns related to money, so I looked inwards each day for several days. Here's an experience that suddenly came to me:

I'm 24 years old, working in a bank in London. They've just done a salary survey and increased our pay so we don't leave and join another bank. Mine has gone up by another 30 per cent. It's increased by 130 per cent since I joined as a graduate trainee two years ago. My mum points out that

I'm earning more than my school headmaster, who's a hero of mine. I'm feeling overpaid. I feel ashamed. I feel I'm being bribed to do something relatively simple – which is becoming boring. There must be more to life than this. A short while later, my girlfriend and I split up. I realize I have a belief that wealth goes together with unhappy relationships. The wealthiest person in my family was my mum's father, with whom I had a lot in common. He made lots of money and was divorced. When I joined the bank in London at the age of 22, there were plenty of divorced people there.

And then another experience came to me:

Now I'm around 10 years old. We refer to my grandad's second wife as our aunt. They live in a grand apartment block overlooking the sea. They often go on cruises and visit exotic places. My grandad occasionally asks my dad, his son-in-law, 'Have you been on a cruise?' Obviously he hasn't. This becomes a standing joke in our family. My parents appear to be happily married, which seems to go with not having much money. Money and divorce seem to go together.

Our family is staying on a caravan site – which Americans would call a trailer park – six miles from our grandad and our aunt. One day they drive over to see us in their Daimler Jaguar. When they leave, my brother and I run alongside the car towards the entrance to the caravan site. She winds down the window and gives us some money before they disappear out of the gate. This happens a few times. I'm pleased with the money, but also feel ashamed.

Now I'm standing outside school with my mum, waiting for my brother who's two years younger than me. I must be six or seven years old. I'm feeling very happy that I've saved up some money in my Post Office account. I start telling someone else's mother about it. My mum intervenes and scolds me for telling other people how much money I have. I conclude there must be something wrong with having money.

As you'll know by now, the solution is simple. We need to re-live – not remember – each incident intensely. Here are some of the incidents I re-lived intensely, over and over again.

- ***'I'm bored at work, but they've raised my salary yet again. I feel I'm being bribed. I feel ashamed.'***
- ***'My grandad asks my dad, "Have you been on a cruise?" I feel sorry for my dad.'***
- ***'My brother and I are running alongside the car. My grandad's second wife winds down the window and gives us some money. Money is nice but I feel guilty about it.'***
- ***'I'm standing outside the school gate. My mum is scolding me for telling people how much money I have. I feel confused and ashamed.'***

Re-living the original incidents removes the pain patterns, which are negative beliefs. Remember:

- **The beliefs in your inner space create each situation in your life.**
- **You don't manifest your desires. You manifest your beliefs.**
- **Once you're complete, your beliefs and desires become one. Then your desires start to manifest.**

The examples of wealth I've given involve money, which is easy to measure but too narrow. Of course, when we lack money and don't know how to manifest more, we're bound to focus on it. But money isn't much use if we're in poor health all the time, and most of our fulfilment involves other people in some way. This can range from direct relationships to knowing that people you've never met are enjoying your book, movie, product or service. The ultimate wealth is knowing that anything is possible, while manifesting whatever you want to happen in your life.

From the age of 20 onwards, I noticed that, when I was excited about what I was doing, money kept pouring in. Sometimes I couldn't figure out where it was all coming from. There have also been long periods when I've been worried about money and chased after it. Predictably, it ran away.

Money is a tool to help you live your life. It's best to focus on fulfilling your potential and serving others. Money follows life.

Now it's your turn

- Write down your earliest painful memories when you came to some negative conclusions about health, wealth or relationships. Use the present tense, as I have in my examples.
- Re-live each episode at least five times, first with your eyes closed, then by talking to yourself in a mirror.

DIG DEEP TO FIND AND COMPLETE WITH YOUR PAIN PATTERNS

Our incompletions are often buried beneath what we say about ourselves, other people, the world and life in general. As an example, here's a conversation I had with a friend who was feeling disturbed by turmoil in the financial markets.

Friend: The world is in a real mess. Most of the politicians are just bonkers. They're pushing the world economy into recession.

Me: Do you feel that something is wrong?

Friend: Yes.

Me: What's your earliest memory of feeling that way?

Friend: I was five years old, growing up in Africa. There was a coup.

Me: That was between the ages of two and seven, so this could lead us to one of the patterns which are running your life. Please become five years old again. What's happening? How do you feel?

Friend: We have to black out the windows and lock all the doors and act as if nobody is at home. I'm peeping out of the curtains at the front window. Men with machine guns are running past our house.

Me: How do you feel? What's your conclusion about yourself, other people, the world and life in general?

Friend: This soon shall pass, and brighter times are ahead for all.

Me: That sounds nice, but you're putting paint on a wound. What did you conclude about yourself, other people, the world and life in general?

Friend: I guess we've got to take off the paint and clean out the muck underneath.

Me: Yes.

Friend: I'm a fighter, a survivor and want to change the world to make it a better place.

Me: That gives us another layer to discover! How did you feel before you declared that you were a fighter, a survivor and wanted to change the world?

Friend: I felt the world was going down.

Me: Great. 'The world is going down' could be one of the five or six pain patterns that are running your life. It could also be part of your root pattern. It's up to you to find out. Please re-live the incident intensely – at least five times – with your eyes closed and then talking to yourself in a mirror. Maybe an earlier incident will come up.

From this example you can see that we often need to dig beneath our statements about ourselves, other people, the world and life in general. Then we can find the pain patterns that are lurking underneath – and complete with them. Once we're complete we make much better decisions – in the financial markets and elsewhere.

Here's another example, with another friend:

Friend: People discriminate against me because of the colour of my skin.

Me: Please go back to the first time you felt you were being discriminated against. What did you conclude about yourself, other people, the world or life in general?

Friend: It isn't fair.

Me: Anything else?

Friend: People are against me.

Me: What are the earliest incidents you can remember when you concluded that 'It isn't fair' or 'People are against me'?

In situations like this, the feeling of being discriminated against can lead us to deeper pain patterns. It's similar to my feeling of not having enough money, which I described earlier. Once I dug deeper I found the pain pattern 'Life doesn't give me what I want'. When I completed with it, a folding bicycle appeared.

HOW TO STOP COMPULSIVE REACTIONS

Most of us react compulsively in certain situations. These are predictable reactions which have become our default setting. Here are some examples:

- **Over-eating when we feel stressed or uncertain – swallowing food suppresses negative emotions for a short while, but then we feel tired and bloated, and put on weight. We don't manifest excellent health.**
- **Getting irritated with people – our frustration comes out at work and in our personal lives. We don't manifest the relationships we want.**
- **Spending money to feel better about ourselves – as with food, this only suppresses our negative emotions briefly. In the meantime, we waste money on things we don't need.**

Compulsive reactions make it hard to manifest our desires in all three dimensions of our lives: health, wealth and relationships. Problems keep showing up in at least one of them. These reactions are unconscious and automatic. Instead of reacting, we need to *respond* in a way that's conscious, intelligent and aware.

Completion is the solution. If you re-live the incidents that gave rise to your pain patterns in the first place, you'll stop reacting compulsively. You'll start *responding* to situations. When something unexpected happens, there's no need to rush. You can unclutch and allow the best response to come to you at the appropriate time. If the situation is urgent, unclutching will help you make the right choice now.

Completion and unclutching will make it far easier to manifest your desires. *Action out of completion leads to more completion.* Life gets better and better.

REPLACE UNCERTAINTY WITH POWERFUL COGNITIONS

If you keep asking 'When will it manifest?', 'Why hasn't it happened yet?', you're expressing uncertainty. You're expressing doubts about your desire manifesting. Progress may grind to a halt.

Some people spend lots of time speculating – 'What if this happens?', 'What if that happens?' They also create doubt by saying things like 'I don't know if it'll work' or 'Do you think this will work?'

I encourage you to drop all this. Work intensely in your chosen direction. The cosmos will manifest at the right time.

If you use the completion technique to make a negative belief redundant, you can then declare a *powerful cognition*. A powerful cognition is the deep understanding and realization that everything we perceive as ourselves is Paramashiva, or Cosmic Consciousness. When we realize this, it transforms our perception of reality and aligns us with the ultimate truth.

Here are two of my favourites:

- **'Life keeps giving me what I need'**
- **'Life is constantly supporting me'**

These great truths reflect the supportive nature of life. Here's another:

- **'It's all happening'**

This powerful cognition acknowledges the inherent intelligence and flow of existence.

By living with these cognitions, we align ourselves with the natural flow of life. They enable us to manifest our desires much more easily.

Completion will make you more intelligent

When we remove our pain patterns – using the completion technique – there can be a big jump in terms of:

- **Comprehension**
- **Memory**
- **Creativity**
- **Intuition**
- **Innovation**

I've experienced this and have seen it in people around me. Unfortunately, while completion makes us more intelligent, incompletion makes us *less* so.

Incompletion can lead to mistaken beliefs and foolish decisions

I enjoy discussing economics and politics on social media and elsewhere. I've noticed that highly intelligent people sometimes refuse to consider data that doesn't fit their existing beliefs, while accepting data that *does* fit. In psychology this is known as *confirmation bias.*

If you let go of any bias and examine data that *doesn't* fit your beliefs, you can formulate a theory that's a much better fit with reality. If you're an investor, this can give you a big advantage and help you make a lot more money. If you're a politician, it can help you win a lot more votes.

There are various theories that attempt to explain confirmation bias. I suggest that incompletion is at least partly responsible. For example, you might have one or more of the following pain patterns:

- **'I'm not intelligent'**
- **'I'm not good enough'**
- **'I keep making mistakes'**

If any of these pain patterns are running your life, you'll avoid data that suggests your opinion is incorrect, since that would trigger your pattern. Unfortunately, you'll be the loser – sooner or later. It's much better to *remove* your pain patterns, using the completion technique. Then you can absorb and use any data that comes your way, from any source.

Actions out of incompletion lead to more incompletion

Most of us aren't aware of our incompletions, so we make decisions and take actions that lead to more incompletion and often more suffering. Here are some examples:

- **You've just emerged from a relationship in which you felt mistreated, but you haven't re-lived the painful incidents to relieve them. You also haven't completed the incidents in your early childhood when you came to negative conclusions or beliefs about yourself, other people, the world and life in general. Remember that you manifest your beliefs, not your desires – so you now attract someone with whom you experience further incompletion and pain.**
- **You feel that one group of people has been unjustly treated, so you try to 'put things right' and 'restore the balance'. You end up treating another group of people unjustly. They object and the conflict begins. We can see this happening in politics, business and social settings. It's a classic example of working on the outside when we should be turning inwards and working on the inside.**
- **You're the president of a country whose people have a long history of suffering. You haven't completed the incidents in your early childhood when you came to conclusions about yourself, other people, the world and life in general. These five or six pain patterns are still running your life. Now the leaders of a neighbouring country do something that triggers your pain patterns. You launch an attack with the support of your citizens. Hundreds of thousands of people are killed or injured on both sides.**

In each of the examples above, the solution is to stop before you take any action. Look inwards:

- **How do you feel?**
- **Where is that feeling in your body?**
- **What's your earliest memory of feeling this way?**
- **What happened? Write it down with a pen, in the first person and the present tense.**
- **Now become that age again. Re-live it intensely, at least five times – firstly with your eyes closed, and secondly while talking to yourself in the mirror.**
- **Allow yourself to feel all the emotions from beginning to end.**

I hope you can see how important it is to complete before you take action! For me it's the top priority. If I feel bad in any way, I stop and look inwards. I find what's bugging me and intensely re-live any painful incident that comes up in my inner space. Once I'm feeling complete, I start taking action again. Action out of completion leads to more completion. Things get better and better.

WE CAN CREATE A BETTER WORLD

While I'm writing this book there's a lot of violence in the world, ranging from physical abuse to gang violence and wars between countries. It's all too easy to label people and take sides. Another common response is to close our eyes and ears – and hope the problems will go away. They won't.

As I explained in chapter 3, each of us is manifesting all the time, so what can we do about this? Here are my recommendations:

- **Make sure you know what's happening in the world, remaining open to information from any source. That way you'll avoid *confirmation bias*, which I described earlier.**
- **Notice when your pain patterns are triggered, then complete with them.**
- **Show others how to find and complete with their pain patterns.**

If we do this we'll reduce the violence in ourselves and in the world. The illusion that we're separate will dissolve.

Find and complete with the pain pattern behind each pattern of behaviour

A pain pattern is not the same as a pattern of behaviour. I was helping a friend with completion when she said she often felt exhausted. Then we got to the root of the problem:

Friend: I'm exhausted.

Me: Why?

Friend: Because I overdo it. I work too hard.

Me: Can you give me an example?

Friend: I charge clients for one hour of my time when I'm working with them. Then I spend several hours following up without charging them. Instead of just sending an email to follow up, I create perfect documents for them. Then I record a video and send it to them.

Me: Why do you do all that, instead of sending an email? What's the belief that's making you do that?

> **Friend: People don't take me seriously.**
>
> **Me: Why don't people take you seriously?**
>
> **Friend: Because I'm unacceptable.**
>
> **Me: When did you conclude that you're unacceptable? What was the original incident?**

As you can see, this pattern of behaviour was leaving my friend exhausted, with little financial reward for her efforts. However, the pain pattern causing the behaviour was much deeper.

Helping others to complete will show you your own pain patterns

When I help others to find their pain patterns and complete with them, I sometimes discover my own patterns. One day I was helping a friend with completion when she realized that one of her patterns was 'This isn't working'.

The following day I spent a lot of time sorting out what should have been a routine international payment. The bank had insisted on using a paper form which hadn't captured all the necessary information. It dawned on me that 'This isn't working' was also part of my reality.

Early the next morning I sat and did completion while the sun came up. I made a list of the areas in my life where I could see that 'This isn't working'. There were 12 of them, ranging from relationships to business to politics. Later in the day I had another go. The list expanded to 24, including the refrigerator, some software on my camera and the electronic door key. I realized I needed to complete with the pattern 'This isn't working'. (I'll come back to this later.)

Completion will remove your fear and greed

For me, letting go of fear and greed has been a complete change of outlook, as it may be for you.

I remember my first economics lesson at school, at the age of 16. The teacher said, 'Economics is the study of the allocation of scarce resources.' The idea of scarcity pervades our culture. If we believe we're separate body/minds, fear and greed follow naturally from this.

We work harder and harder to get money. Then we hoard it because we're afraid that no more will come. We also try to manipulate other people by exploiting *their* fear and greed. Fear reduces our energy and limits our perception. Greed creates a constant feeling of lack.

When we complete with our pain patterns, we let go of fear and greed. Then we naturally attract people and situations that reflect our new inner space. We don't need to chase or struggle. Life unfolds effortlessly around us.

Let go of fear and greed at work and in your relationships

Many of us have been conditioned to get a job and please our boss. I remember a phrase from the prospectus for the Cambridge economics course: 'Our graduates have no difficulty securing interesting and well-paid employment.' No mention of being self-employed or starting a business. Just get a job and please your boss.

More recently it dawned on me that I was trying and failing to please several people at once. I felt stuck in several hierarchies. I was unable to meet – simultaneously – the expectations of everyone who felt I should be reporting to them. If you consider your own situation, you may find it looks like the diagram below. You're in two, three – maybe more – hierarchies at the same time:

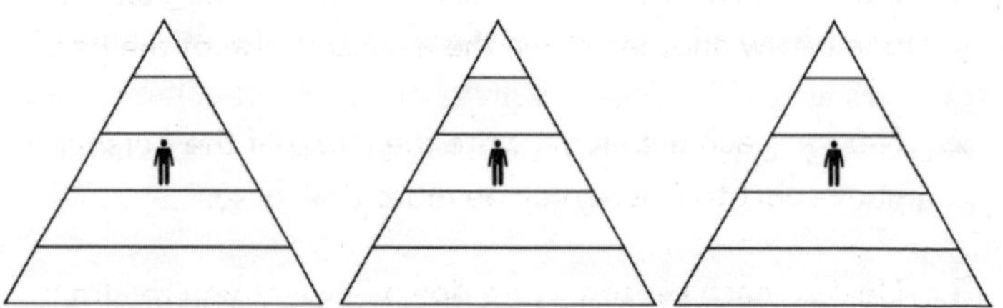

Here are some hierarchies in which you may find yourself:

- **Job**
- **Business**
- **Family**
- **Voluntary organization**
- **Spiritual community**
- **Political party**
- **Sports team**

I could feel the stress in my body as I tried to achieve goals that other people had set for me. Eventually, I realized I was doing this out of fear and greed. I was afraid of being excluded or punished if I didn't meet their expectations. I was hoping for some reward if I *did* meet them.

Now it's your turn

Take a pen and a piece of paper:

1. Make a list of the hierarchies in which you find yourself, one below another, down the left-hand side of the page.

2. Next to each hierarchy, write the name of the person you report to (there may be more than one).

3. Next to each person, write down (a) what you're afraid of, and (b) what you hope to gain from them.

4. Write down how you feel about this situation.

I also realized that most or all of these people were setting goals for me and others out of incompletion. (Once we see the incompletions in ourselves, it's easier to see them in other people.) For example, many leaders are convinced that something is wrong and keep trying to put it right. This often involves trying to fix other people, most of whom don't want to be fixed.

Instead of seeing ourselves as separate body/minds in multiple hierarchies, it's much better to see ourselves at the centre of concentric circles – as shown in the diagram below:

The inner circles are likely to include your family and close friends. Further out will be your colleagues and acquaintances. The outer circles will include people you pass in the street without meeting them, then people you never even see. In my case there are people who read my books in languages I don't understand. In your case it could be someone who uses your product, or listens to your music, or benefits in some other way from what you do.

If you think about the people in these concentric circles, they're affected by:

- **What you say**
- **What you do**
- **What you eat**
- **What you drink**
- **How you vote**
- **How you travel**
- **How you spend your money**
- **What you write on social media**
- **How you behave when no one's looking**

You're constantly having an impact on the whole world – way beyond what you can see around you. It's like throwing a stone into a pond. The ripples – whether positive or negative – radiate throughout the world. By taking responsibility for your actions, you help to create a better world.

If you keep practising completion, you'll let go of your fear and greed. You'll keep radiating positive thoughts, emotions and actions. The world mirrors your inner state, and will respond to you accordingly. If you radiate positivity, you'll attract similar responses and experiences. You'll manifest more of what you want and less of what you don't want. We'll focus on this in the next chapter.

SUMMARY

- If you complete with your pain patterns you can succeed in all areas of your life and stop your pain patterns from messing up your life.
- You can stop compulsive reactions, which make it hard to manifest your desires.
- If you replace uncertainty with powerful cognitions, manifesting will become easier.
- Completion will make you more intelligent, while incompletion can lead to mistaken beliefs and foolish decisions. Actions out of incompletion lead to more incompletion.
- You can create a better world. Helping others to complete will show you your own pain patterns.
- Completion will remove your fear and greed. You can let go of fear and greed at work and in your relationships.
- Instead of seeing yourself as a separate body/mind, it's much better to see yourself at the centre of concentric circles. The people in these concentric circles are affected by everything you do.
- If you radiate positivity, you'll attract similar responses and experiences.

6

DECIDE TO MANIFEST YOUR DESIRES

Most people are trying to manifest their desires in one way or another. Sometimes they succeed, sometimes they don't. The reason for the patchy results is that we don't manifest our *desires*. We manifest our *beliefs*.

As I've described previously, pain patterns – or negative beliefs – are running your life. You keep manifesting what you believe about yourself, other people, the world and life in general.

In order to manifest your desires, you need to close the gap between your beliefs and your desires. That's what completion does. When your belief matches your desire, the desire manifests – sometimes in an unexpected way.

In this chapter, we're going to start the process of manifesting. Remember that whatever we hold in our inner space starts manifesting. I'm going to show you how to do this. My experience is that sometimes I need to take action, sometimes I don't. In any event, my intuition tells me what to do.

Create the space to manifest your desires

Whatever we hold in our inner space starts manifesting. I'm going to show you how to do this.

This is how to *create the space*, in five steps:

1. **Choose something you want to manifest.**
2. **Create the space for it. Space creation is 'bringing your future possibility into the present':**

- **Visualize it in the present**
- **Think about it, using words**
- **Feel and cognize that it's already a reality**

3. **Now listen carefully to your thoughts and write them down. They're showing you the pain patterns that are preventing you from manifesting your desire. Complete with all of them, including any self-doubt or impossibilities, following the instructions on page 60.**
4. **After completing, go back to step 2 and re-create the space inside you.**
5. **Keep doing this until you're able to create the space for your chosen reality without any incompletions coming up.**

If you follow these steps carefully, your desires will manifest much faster and more easily than before. The completion technique closes the gap between your belief and your desire. Then your desire manifests.

The process of creating the space shows us where we're stuck. We need to look inwards, find the pain pattern and then re-live the original incident intensely.

Here are some examples of incompletion, self-doubt and impossibility that may appear in your inner space during step 3:

- **'I'm too old'**
- **'I'm too young'**
- **'I'm not good enough'**
- **'I'm unacceptable'**
- **'I'm not intelligent enough'**
- **'I don't know enough'**
- **'I'm ugly'**
- **'I'm a failure'**
- **'People don't support me'**
- **'It isn't fair'**

- **'Life is unfair'**
- **'Something is wrong'**
- **'Life doesn't give me what I want'**
- **'I'm not getting what I want'**
- **'It's impossible'**

Impossibility patterns appear in many forms. For example, businesspeople may say, 'The market is bad' or 'There's a crisis in the economy' – and then go on to say that something is impossible.

Completion will remove your impossibility patterns. In chapter 4 I gave the example of manifesting a Brompton folding bicycle. When I completed with my pattern of 'It's impossible', the bicycle appeared.

After I learned to 'create the space', I began to show other people how to do it. At that time, a friend of mine was looking for a job – and getting very frustrated. He had lots of bills to pay and was running short of money. This is how he described the experience to me recently:

'You and I spoke every day for a couple of weeks. I found several pain patterns, like "I'm not good enough" and "I don't deserve it". I re-lived the incidents intensely, as you asked me to.

'In the space of 48 hours I manifested three job offers. Two of them weren't that high in terms of salary. The third offer was the salary I was looking for, so I accepted it. That's the job I have now.'

It's good to work on completion with a buddy. You can help each other to find your blindspots – the pain patterns that are preventing each of you from manifesting your desires.

What about past failures?

Some of us have failed so many times that we've just about given up hope. When I worked in sales – before I learned to be present and surrender – I used to set a target every month and then fail to meet it. This was despite detailed action plans and an intense motivation to succeed.

If you've also experienced multiple failures, I have some good news for you. Your past failures weren't due to lack of intelligence. You failed in the past because you didn't have the right space.

If you change your space, as I'm describing in this chapter, your results will change for the better. If you also ask the Cosmic Intelligence to manifest through you – as I'll describe later in this book – your life will be transformed.

Work on one desire at a time

If you focus on one desire with clarity, other desires will manifest simultaneously. This is because manifesting isn't just about achieving a particular goal – it's about tuning into the Cosmic Intelligence. When you focus on one desire, the cosmos responds by fulfilling multiple desires in alignment with your intentions.

Now that I've described the technique for manifesting, we can focus on health, wealth and relationships. Let's start with . . .

MANIFESTING HEALTH

How do you want to improve your health? Please write down what you want to manifest.

Not everyone wants to hear this, but many of our ailments can be traced back to our thoughts and behaviours. Let's take the example of being overweight. Many people want to be slimmer, healthier – or both – but they find themselves overeating, or eating compulsively. The first step is to look inwards to find your earliest memories of doing this. Here are a couple of mine:

> *I'm seven or eight years old, on holiday with my brothers and our parents. We're in a restaurant with my grandfather and his wife. The adults are pleased when I order and consume an adult portion. They say it will make me big and strong. It's a lot of food, but I just about manage it. The grown-ups seem pleased with me now. They approve.*

> *I'm a trainee with Europe's largest independent fund management firm. I've concluded that I can't do this job. It requires intuition as well as analysis. My intuition seems to have died during years of intellectual activity. I can't see a way out. The only other job I'm interested in – recruitment – requires even more intuition. The jobs for which I'm well qualified – investment banking and management consultancy – fill me with dread. I feel trapped and powerless. Something is wrong. I feel like a failure. I've also been diagnosed with clinical depression. I keep waking up early – full of worries – and then feel exhausted for the rest of the day. I'm on my way home, standing on the platform as usual. Sometimes I feel like jumping under a train. Today I turn my attention to a kiosk which sells newspapers, snacks and chocolate bars. I buy a Cadbury Caramel chocolate bar. It's divided up into segments, each of which contains caramel. I eat the whole bar quickly.*

Re-living these episodes intensely has helped me to keep my weight down. I encourage you to find and re-live your earliest memories of any pattern that's damaging for your health.

MANIFESTING WEALTH

What do you want to manifest in terms of wealth? Please write it down now.

Many of us want to be wealthy – or at least wealthier than we are now – but we do things that destroy wealth. Over a period of several years I made investments in a dozen early-stage companies. In each case I lost some or all of my money.

There was clearly a pattern, so I looked inwards. I realized I was investing my money in other people's businesses because I believed I couldn't manifest wealth myself.

- **I was afraid of missing out on the next multibillion-dollar company.**
- **I was blind to the founders' pain patterns that were causing them to fail.**

I looked inwards to find the source of my behaviour. Here are some of the incidents I found:

I'm working in sales and marketing. Every month I set a target which I fail to achieve. I feel like a failure.

I'm 27 years old, working hard to build a company that licenses software to financial advisors. I hope to become a millionaire but it doesn't work out, so I feel like a failure.

This takes me back to the age of six when I fail my colour-blindness test and conclude that I'm a failure.

My earliest memory of feeling that I'm missing out is at the age of seven. The other boys don't want me in the soccer team, so I stay indoors, drawing and writing poetry.

I've just left business school and want to work in recruitment, but my intuition seems to have died. I conclude that I can't 'read' other people.

Having re-lived each incident intensely, I felt much better. These days I work with companies whose founders or CEOs complete, unclutch and surrender.

I encourage you to look inwards and find any patterns that are destroying your wealth. Then find the original incidents and re-live them intensely to relieve them.

Once we've stopped destroying our wealth, we're well-placed to manifest more of it. Our beliefs attract people and situations. Our wealth is a reflection of what we hold in our inner space – whether it's pain patterns or powerful cognitions.

I've met many hard-working people who struggle with wealth. Most don't realize that they're manifesting their beliefs, not their desires. Some do realize, but they haven't yet done the work to discover and complete with their pain patterns.

One of the best ways to manifest wealth is to share your talents with the world. We all have talents – perhaps in some unique combination – but we often take them for granted, or assume that everyone can do what comes to us naturally.

For example, when I graduated I assumed that everyone who was educated could write clearly. Then I joined a bank and discovered that wasn't the case. At one point I was being very well paid to write documents which explained transactions to clients in plain English – with a few diagrams. It seemed obvious to me, but my colleagues valued it highly.

How about you?

What do you do naturally, and enjoy doing? How can that benefit other people? Maybe you assume that everyone can do it – but they can't. Maybe you do it in some unique way that other people value.

You may have one or more talents that have nothing to do with your education. Many of us are engaged in activities that didn't exist when we were at school or university.

It doesn't matter how old you are. You can still discover talents that you didn't know you had. If you keep experimenting and trying new things, you'll discover them.

What action should you take?

So, what action should you take to manifest wealth? As I mentioned earlier, action may or may not be necessary to manifest your desires:

- **In some cases, all we need to do is hold the desire in our inner space and complete with any pain patterns that are preventing it from manifesting.**

- **In other cases, we need to take action externally as well. The question is, what action? Most of us don't want to waste time going up one blind alley after another.**

I strongly recommend focusing on creating the space to manifest your desires. Then do whatever your intuition tells you to do. That may include work, which will be highly productive.

Here's a famous verse from the *Bhagavad Gita*, a Hindu scripture, where Krishna – an eternal manifestation of the Divine – says to his friend, Arjuna:

> *'Do your actions dropping all attachment to the outcome,*
> *being centered and complete in Yoga.*
> *Be balanced in success and failure. Such evenness of mind is Yoga.'*[10]

Krishna is talking about acting from the space of completion, which I described earlier. We let go of any attachment to the result and do what we have to do. I find this refreshing and highly productive. My intuition tells me what to do (for example, write this book). Then I immerse myself in it, without worrying about the results.

You may be wondering about the use of the word *yoga*. It's often seen as a physical activity, but it goes far deeper than that. *Yoga* can be translated from Sanskrit to English as 'union'. Yoga is intended to unite the individual consciousness with the universal consciousness – as I'm describing in this book. Letting go of our attachment to the outcome helps us to remain in the space of completion. Then our true desires manifest easily.

Many of us have been conditioned to do the opposite: focus on results. This is common in business, particularly in companies that report their earnings to investors at regular intervals. Once we focus on results – instead of the activity itself – we can easily find ourselves trying to control everything. We're driven by fear and greed.

Don't think about the results

Have you been in situations where you focused on results? Have you been in other situations where you focused on the activity itself? What was the difference for you? How did it feel? What happened?

My experience is that the best results have usually come when I *wasn't* thinking about the results. In most cases, I wasn't thinking about anything except the activity itself. I was immersed in it. I can see this in my studies, in writing, photography, executive search – and when I'm helping people to complete.

MANIFESTING RELATIONSHIPS

As I said earlier, most of us have been conditioned to see ourselves as separate body/minds, among billions of other body/minds. We also tend to see each other as fixed. In describing our relationship with someone, we often say that she's like this or he's like that. We accumulate evidence to support our fixed view of the other person – with all their quirks and defects. If we carry on like this, we're likely to find the other person more and more annoying. Managing the relationship becomes tiring and stressful. Maybe we hold it together just long enough to get the job done. There are many couples who divorce just as their youngest child leaves home. Another example is business partners or political allies who separate – then damage or destroy what they've been building together.

Please remember that the people around you are a reflection of you – an extension of you. At the deepest level there's no separation. They *are* you.

Five steps for manifesting happy, harmonious relationships

1. Listen At one point I realized I was listening carefully to some people but not others. When I was talking to people I'd disagreed with many times, I would half-listen politely, having already decided that I wouldn't be following their advice. So I decided to start listening carefully to everyone.

The more carefully we listen to people, the better our relationship with them. The more you listen to yourself and others, the more you'll inspire them to listen to you.

I find that completion and unclutching really help me to listen. When I'm complete I don't have lots of random thoughts bubbling up in my inner space. I can unclutch from any that *do* appear.

I can just relax and listen. There's no need to think while I'm listening. Anything that needs to be said will come to me after the other person has finished speaking.

2. Notice your pain patterns and complete with them Many of us discover our incompletions *while listening*. Someone says something that triggers one of our pain patterns. Then we stop listening.

As soon as you have the opportunity, I recommend you sit and listen to *yourself*, so you can find the original incident when you came to a particular conclusion about yourself, other people, the world or life in general. Please write down a description of the incident – in the present tense – as you did for health and wealth. Write down how you *feel* about what's happening. Re-live the incident intensely at least five times with your eyes closed and then again five times while talking to yourself in the mirror. *Feel* all the emotions that come up.

Once you're complete you'll be able to listen to people without that particular pain pattern being triggered. If something does disturb you, I recommend you unclutch from it and keep listening.

While you're listening, you may detect other people's pain patterns – which can be a reflection of your own. At the deepest level, when you're listening to other people, you're listening to yourself. There's no separation.

If you complete with your pain patterns, your relationships will change for the better. If you complete with your *root pattern*, your relationships will be transformed.

3. Let go of baggage from the past Romantic relationships are a good example. Many people conduct a forensic analysis of their last relationship, hoping things will work out better next time. They think about how their ex behaved, and then resolve to avoid 'that kind of person' in future. Or they analyse their own behaviour and resolve to 'do better next time'. We can spend years on this kind of analysis and get nowhere. The same principle applies to other types of relationship – with friends, colleagues, bosses, clients and customers.

Our relationships reflect the pain patterns that are running our lives. If you want a fulfilling relationship, the best thing you can do is to find and complete with your pain patterns. They may include beliefs such as 'I'm not good enough', or 'People exploit me'. There are other permutations. Any one of them can prevent you from manifesting your desired relationships.

4. Complete with others If the other person is available, please complete with them directly, face to face – either in person or via video. If they aren't available, you can complete with a photograph of them. This will deeply heal your inner space.

Here's how to complete with others:

1. **Resolve not to hold any incompletions and to drop all negative patterns related to them.**
2. **Talk to the other person. Describe your incompletion and explain that you're taking full responsibility for it. (You aren't blaming them for anything. The pain pattern that's being triggered is in *you*.)**
3. **Help them to fulfil their desires and aspirations.**

These three steps will resolve your issues with other people. You'll develop harmonious and supportive relationships.

Here's an example of completion with others. Earlier I mentioned the time when my mum put me in the barber's chair, so he could cut my hair. I felt powerless and extremely frustrated.

While writing this book I was experiencing difficulties in my relationship with a colleague. I wasn't the only one. There was a lot of blame and finger-pointing going on in our team. (It's easy to fall into this trap when we treat each other as separate.)

When I looked inwards, I had a strong feeling that she was bossing me around. Then I found the pain pattern that was being triggered every time she asked me to do something. The original incident was in the barber's chair.

I spoke to her and explained about my pain pattern being triggered. Obviously, I had to take responsibility for it, since the pain pattern was in my body – and had been since the age of three. We both laughed about it and I focused on re-living the incident to relieve it. That improved our relationship a lot. After that, whenever she asked me to do something, I said yes or no. I was no longer triggered every time she asked.

5. Help the people around you to complete At first, not everyone will be open to completion, but some will become curious when they see the change in you. One of my former colleagues said he was amazed I'd never got annoyed with him, even when he'd deliberately provoked me several times. People will also notice that you're triggered by external events much less than before.

Some people resist completion for a while, even if they know it works for me. They still come to me with their problems. I listen carefully, but don't get involved in any drama. Instead, I focus on the spiritual solution by asking the following questions:

- **How do you feel?**
- **What's your earliest memory of feeling this way? What's the original incident?**
- **What did you conclude about yourself, other people, the world and life in general?**

Then I show them how to complete: how to re-live the original incident in order to remove the pain pattern that's being triggered in the current situation.

Being complete while surrounded by people who also practise completion makes life easy and enjoyable.

Practise perpetual completion

I recommend you practise completion every morning or evening. If you want to change your life quickly, do both.

Within a month you'll acquire a taste for completion. Perpetual completion will change your inner space. The people around you will change – as will the situations in which you find yourself. You'll also attract new people into your life.

Complete the painful incidents that occurred before you had any vocabulary

Once you've re-lived an incident intensely, an earlier one may come up. As you go back further and further, you may find that the first time you felt powerless was before you had any vocabulary – it could be a feeling or a mood that you can recall. We need to complete with this feeling. Metaphorically speaking, we need to boil the land, so no patterns can grow.

Once when I turned inwards, I had a deep feeling of insecurity. I could see how this feeling had continued throughout my life, up until now. For several days I re-lived the feeling. I sat and felt it five times with my eyes closed. Then I talked to myself in the mirror, describing how I felt five times. Suddenly I remembered being one or two years old.

> *I'm lying in my cot – or crib, as Americans call it. I'm screaming and screaming.*

Then I remember a later incident.

> *I'm seven and my youngest brother is only a few months old. When he cries, my dad says we should let him continue. It will make him stronger.*

Presumably that's what happened to me when I was a baby. I decide to give it a try and re-live it.

> *I'm one or two years old, lying in my cot in the dark. I scream and scream, but nobody comes.*

I re-lived this experience over and over again, one day after another. I knew it was a real experience because I could feel the pain in the centre of my chest.

Once I'd identified this pain pattern, I began to notice when it was triggered in everyday situations. One example was listening to executives who were discriminating among employees on the basis of their sex or skin colour. Another was listening to politicians who were trying to mislead voters. In both cases I felt that something was wrong.

Many people have the feeling that something is wrong. I'm not just talking about social justice or democratic values. I'm talking about a deep sense that things are not the way they should be. If you have this feeling, it will manifest in many areas of your life.

The notion that something was wrong came up frequently during my childhood. My dad often asked, 'What's wrong?' Some people say this comes from our evolution as a species. Imagine you're living in a cave, surrounded by dangerous animals. (There are very few humans, so there are lots more animals.) As a cave person you're constantly scanning your environment to see what's wrong. Is a tiger approaching my cave? Is the forest on fire? Does someone in my family have an illness – for which there's no cure?

Early each morning I wore my earplugs with my eyes closed. I re-lived the episode in my cot at the age of one.

I'm one or two years old, lying in my cot in the dark. I scream and scream, but nobody comes. After a while the re-living feels like a mantra – a gentle throbbing in my head. I have a feeling of powerlessness in my legs and arms, as well as the usual dull ache in the centre of my chest. I keep re-living, over and over again. Sometime later the bodily sensations stop, and there's only silence, followed by bliss for no reason.

It's like someone switching off a radio playing in the background. Most of the time there's a perpetual loop of the same old tunes, the same old negative stories. Suddenly it stops. Now I can hear what's going on around me.

Then a new cognition comes to me: 'Life is constantly giving me what I need'. It continues to reverberate inside me. Later it becomes 'Life is constantly supporting me'. I know this is a huge change.

It reverberates in my inner space. Now I see how life has always supported me, clearing the way for me to take the next step.

Don't play the victim

When things aren't working out the way we want, many of us resort to playing the victim. It's a way of telling ourselves that what we're doing is right – and getting support from other people.

While playing the victim may provide some comfort in the short term, it prevents us from looking inwards and finding the pain patterns that are running our lives. This principle applies to individuals, families, social groups and countries. There are many examples of one country playing the victim prior to attacking or invading another.

The best starting point for all of us is to look inwards. Are you blaming other people instead of looking inwards and finding the pain pattern that's causing this situation?

Sometimes we play the victim when we're expecting too many things to happen, too quickly. It's better to relax and unclutch. Let go of your attachment to the outcome. Just keep working in the desired direction and allow the results to come at the appropriate time.

In any event, there's no way you can be a victim. You're Supreme Consciousness, Paramashiva. If you turn inwards, find your pain patterns and complete with them, you'll start manifesting your desires.

If something isn't working, it's for a reason

When we run into an obstacle, we have a choice. One option is to become powerless. The second option is to unclutch from any thoughts or emotions that come up, then look inwards.

I've frequently been in situations where something wasn't working. Eventually I realized that something much bigger was trying to happen. Here are three examples from everyday life:

- **A business goes into liquidation. The founder then starts another which has far more potential.**
- **Your partner leaves you. Sometime later a more suitable person appears.**
- **You fail to get a particular job, then something much better happens.**

Having recruited chief executives and chief financial officers, I've met plenty of people who were turned down for one job – and then became very successful and wealthy in another.

Make sure you're complete before you make decisions or take action

In chapter 5, I described how actions out of incompletion lead to more incompletion.

Our pain patterns can be triggered at any time and lead to painful outcomes. For example, I once worked with an entrepreneur whose pain patterns included 'I can't trust other people'. As a result he made two decisions. The first was not to sign a shareholders' agreement. The second was to fire his board of directors. As a result, he couldn't raise any money and the business went nowhere.

If you make sure you're complete before you make decisions and take action, you'll be much more successful. For me, staying complete is the top priority. If I feel incomplete about anything, I sit down and listen to myself. I complete before I make any major decisions or embark on any course of action.

Look for the incompletions behind your desires

When I'm helping people to manifest their desires, some of them tell me they want this or that qualification, from this or that institution. I ask them why.

If you have a genuine desire to study a particular subject, there shouldn't be a problem. However, many people want a certain qualification on their CV because they feel something is wrong. I ask them how they feel about themselves, other people, the world and life in general. Here are some of their responses:

- **'I'm not intelligent enough.'**
- **'People don't respect me.'**
- **'Other people are smarter than me.'**

Getting a certificate may only bolster the image you present to the outside world. In the meantime you'll continue feeling bad about yourself and nothing much will change. If you find your pain patterns and complete with them, you can manifest extraordinary things. You may not need any more certificates.

COMPLETE WITH YOUR PATTERN OF IMPOSSIBILITY

In chapter 4 I described how I concluded – at the age of six – that it was impossible for me to join the armed forces or fly aeroplanes. The optometrist told me and I believed him. He had a physical reason: I was partially red-green colour blind. When I grew up I had no interest in being a soldier or a pilot, but the pattern of impossibility stayed with me, until I completed with it.

In the meantime I worked with a man who was at least as colour blind as I was. He'd served in the army with the Corps of Royal Electrical and Mechanical Engineers, where he worked on rocket systems. This made me laugh. Life was showing how my beliefs had been limiting me. Presumably my colleague didn't believe in impossibility the way I did at that time.

Our impossibility patterns often appear as generalizations

Our belief in impossibility is noticeable when we generalize. Here are some examples:

- **'I've never been good with money.'**
- **'I'm hopeless at languages.'**
- **'I'm no good at mathematics.'**

- **'Other people can't be trusted.'**
- **'Life is hard.'**

All five of these statements are beliefs. Remember, you manifest your beliefs, not your desires.

In order to manifest your desires, you need to look inwards and find the original incidents when you came to negative conclusions about yourself, other people, the world and life in general. Then you can re-live those incidents to relieve any pain patterns that are preventing your desires from manifesting.

ALLOW YOUR DESIRES TO MANIFEST IN THE BEST WAY

Many of us have fixed ideas about how our desires are going to manifest. Then we get upset or depressed when things don't work out the way we expected. If we step back, we can see this approach makes no sense. The cosmos is ultra-intelligent, constantly manifesting in ways beyond our logic. We may dream up a series of steps that we *think* will get us from A to B, but there's no reason why the cosmos should follow them.

The solution is simple: be clear about *what* you're manifesting and allow it to manifest in the best way. Once you've created the space for your desire to manifest, leave the result to the cosmos. Let go of any fixed ideas about how it's going to happen.

Imagine you're sitting on a beach and you see a lighthouse on a headland several miles away. You have a desire to visit the lighthouse. Now you use your mind and start planning how to get there. You identify three options: you consult the bus timetable, you estimate how long it would take to walk, you find out how much it costs to take a taxi.

Doing your homework is fine, but at the same time, it's best to be open-minded about *how* your desire will manifest. If you create the space as I described earlier in this chapter, then anything can happen. Maybe someone will give you a lift in their car. Maybe they'll pick you up in their speed boat or helicopter. Our desires can manifest much faster than we imagine, often in ways that never occur to us if we only use our minds.

Manifesting over the long term

Here's a personal example of desires manifesting in the best way over the long term. As I mentioned in my earlier book, *The Power of Letting Go*, when I was a student I decided not to write any books. I couldn't see the point – there were millions of them already.

My first job after university was in banking. I worked in several departments and completed my training in London and Chicago. It was interesting and enjoyable, but I realized in my early twenties that I wanted to help change the world.

I considered charities and politics as vehicles for changing the world. It was exciting to join a new political party which looked as though it was going to have a big impact, but it didn't. In the meantime I decided to go to business school and explore other options.

Like many people, I soon became clear about what I *didn't* want – and struggled with that for years. But the desire to help change the world didn't go away.

A few years later I was working for one of the world's largest executive search firms. I met lots of candidates who were looking for new jobs. Most of them didn't seem to understand how executive search worked, or how to market themselves to people like me. No one had explained it to them. Having given the same advice to many candidates, my colleague Barbara Edlmair and I decided to write a book which would explain it to them. A publisher quickly made an offer for *How To Be Headhunted*, which sold several thousand copies.

I then realized that lots of other people needed to market themselves more broadly – and not just via headhunters. I met David Royston-Lee and we wrote *Brand You*, which sold tens of thousands of copies in multiple languages.

In the meantime I'd been practising mindfulness and Transcendental Meditation. Then I met Swamiji and began to learn further techniques from the Vedic tradition. I wanted to share what I'd learned with as many people as possible. *The Power of Letting Go* has sold hundreds of thousands of copies so far.

My aim now is to help millions of people – including you. I never decided to write bestsellers. I started writing to help people. Everything unfolded from there. In short, my mind was wrong about writing books.

Here's another example of unexpected outcomes. A friend of mine, Mark O'Sullivan, was sexually abused as a child. He later wrote and directed *My Sexual Abuse: The Sitcom*, for which he was presented with a Royal Television Society award in the UK. This is what he says:

'I've realized two things in the last few years. Firstly, that when I'm completely immersed in whatever it is I'm doing – writing, directing, acting, sometimes a combination of all three – I feel a complete absence of fear and anxiety, and seem to know exactly what to do and when to do it. This is usually coupled with a feeling of focus and excitement. I think some people call this state 'flow'. Whatever it is, whatever it's called, it's my favourite space to occupy.

'My other realization is that whenever I've experienced my biggest failures, or hardest, most challenging moments, they've always been followed by a surge of energy. I think of it as like a huge tidal wave – it can consume me, drive me down further into the water, or I can harness it. Ride the wave. I've usually had my biggest successes in life straight after these hardest moments.

'In both cases, I don't know where the energy or state is going to take me. This used to terrify me – but I know now that to not know is liberating. It means anything is possible, not just the narrow band of outcomes I'd previously think should be the end result.'

Your inner space is the most important factor in manifesting your desires

As I described earlier, there may be little or no correlation between effort and results:

- **You can put an enormous effort into something that doesn't happen.**
- **Equally, you may put little or no effort into something that manifests quickly and easily.**

A good place to observe this is in sales. You may have heard people say that 'sales is a numbers game'. Many people assume that the probability of someone saying 'yes' is fixed. Having made this assumption, they bang on lots of doors – metaphorically or physically – hoping that someone will open the door, welcome them and buy something. However, the success rate in sales varies hugely from one person to another. Some people knock on a hundred doors and no one buys anything. Others knock on a hundred doors and twenty people buy something. Having observed sales people over many years, I would say their success rate is a function of their beliefs, not their desires.

Here's an example from another field – literally. A monk from a Buddhist community was walking on Hampstead Heath in North London when he was approached by a man who was out jogging. The jogger said he'd read an article in the local newspaper about the monk's community, who wanted to live in a forest. He said he owned 140 acres (57 hectares) of forest in southern England. Long story short: he gave it to them.

What can we learn from the monk? Some people conclude that they should spend more time walking on Hampstead Heath. Others dismiss this episode as coincidence. (As I said earlier, 'coincidence' means two things happen at the same time – it doesn't mean it's random.) My experience is that, the more I complete, unclutch and feel grateful, the more frequently these helpful coincidences occur. My desires manifest much faster and more easily.

RAISE THE LEVEL OF YOUR CONSCIOUSNESS

The higher the level of our consciousness, the more easily we manifest. We can sail over any obstacles. Hence the Zen proverb, 'The obstacle is the path.'

One metaphor for levels of consciousness is a building with a hundred floors. Many of us are on the ground floor, where we can't see very much. There are hedges in the way, and flies that bother us. Now imagine you're on the hundredth floor. You can see for miles and miles. What looks like a big problem when you're on the ground floor looks very different from the higher floors.

I can say from experience that depression is in the basement. (If you haven't been down there already, there's no need to go and see for yourself.) Depression showed me that I needed to move on from the mind to Cosmic Intelligence. That experience has also enabled me to write books that will help millions of people.

Many times I've tried to manifest something that wasn't working. When I finally let go – by completing and unclutching – something bigger and more fulfilling happened.

When I talk to people about what's happening in their lives, I often hear the word 'setback' – as though everything was going fine until they ran into some obstacle. I'm telling you that the obstacle is the way forward. You need to go up a level in order to move forwards and fulfil your potential.

Unclutching and completion will raise the level of your consciousness. The higher you go, the more frequently you'll experience helpful coincidences. Manifestation will become easier.

Another metaphor that's sometimes used for manifesting is higher and lower frequencies – or vibrations. As the saying goes, 'Your vibe attracts your tribe.' As you raise your frequency, you attract different people. It becomes easier to manifest your desires.

It isn't immediately obvious how this principle can be tested under controlled conditions. There are hundreds if not thousands of variables in our daily lives. But you don't need a laboratory. You can deliberately raise the level of your consciousness and see what happens in your daily life.

Try for yourself

Please do the following:

- Practise completion at least once a day.
- Unclutch over and over again throughout the day.
- Be grateful for everything that manifests – no matter how big or small.
- Notice how your life changes.
- Write down your experiences as a reminder.

In this chapter I've described how to use spiritual techniques to manifest your desires much more easily. In the next chapter I'll explain how the Cosmic Intelligence can manifest through you.

SUMMARY

- You don't manifest what you desire, but you manifest what you believe.
- Accepting yourself isn't enough – you have to complete with your pain patterns.
- You don't achieve what you work for. You achieve what you hold the space for.
- If you work on one desire at a time, other desires will manifest simultaneously.
- Many of our ailments can be traced back to our thoughts and behaviours.
- Our wealth is a reflection of what we hold in our inner space. One of the best ways to manifest wealth is to share your talents with the world.
- Action may or may not be necessary to manifest your desires.
- Letting go of your attachment to the outcome helps you to remain in the space of completion. Then your true desires manifest easily.
- The people around you are a reflection of you – an extension of you. At the deepest level there's no separation. They *are* you.
- If something isn't working, it's for a reason.
- Many of us have a pattern of impossibility. These impossibility patterns often appear as generalizations.

- Your inner space is the most important factor in manifesting your desires.
- You need to raise the level of your consciousness to make manifestation easier.

7

BECOME A PURE CHANNEL

We have a choice:

- **Option 1 is to keep analysing and solving each problem that comes up.**
- **Option 2 is to surrender to the intelligence that's running the cosmos. That intelligence will then manifest through you and fulfil your desires.**

Maybe you've never made this choice consciously before. As you'll know by now, most of us have been conditioned to believe that we're separate body/minds in a world governed by the laws of classical physics. So we choose option 1 by default. We see ourselves as a separate body/mind with certain abilities, disabilities, achievements, qualifications, limitations and relationships. Then we keep on thinking. We compare what's happening now with what happened in the past. We try to anticipate what will happen in the future. It's exhausting. We do all this because we see ourselves as separate.

The second option dawned on me one morning when I was doing yoga in Swamiji's ashram near Bangalore, India. The *acharya* (instructor) said, 'Become a pure channel.'

If you become a pure channel, the Cosmic Intelligence can manifest anything through you. The way to do this is to complete, unclutch and surrender.

You can manifest without thinking

Maybe you've had the experience of manifesting without thinking. It happens when we're complete and unclutched.

Thoughts come from incompletions and disturbances in our inner space. When we're complete and unclutched we enter the state of *nirvikalpa samadhi*, which can be translated as 'unwavering oneness with the source'. It's a thoughtless state of existence. You don't need to rely on thoughts to function or respond to situations. You act spontaneously from the space of completion. You're aligned with the Cosmic Intelligence, the natural flow of existence.

My experience is that I know what to do next. Sometimes I even receive an instruction to do something next. I've learned to follow that instruction. You can experience this for yourself if you complete and unclutch.

Leave the timing to the cosmos

When I worked in sales and marketing, I met people who were very keen on goal-setting, which usually included an action plan and a deadline by which something was supposed to happen. When I look back, it makes me laugh. The plan almost never became reality. Something else usually happened instead. Or sometimes it happened much faster, in an unexpected way.

It's great to be clear about your desires. I've devoted a whole chapter to that. But once we tune into the Cosmic Intelligence, it's best to leave the timing to that intelligence.

Look back on your life

Can you recall something that happened later than you anticipated – and the delay proved to be very helpful in the long term? We may not see it at the time, but it becomes obvious later.

Maybe you can recall a time when you had a fixed idea about when something was going to happen. Then you let go and it happened *faster or in another way.*

EGO

Becoming a pure channel means being free from ego, expectations and the notion of the separate self. Allow me to explain.

Ego is the Latin word for 'I'. However, East and West view ego in different ways. In Western culture, some people say they have 'a healthy ego'. Many of us see the ego as something useful that just needs to be managed. Here are some examples:

- **'She has her ego under control.'**
- **'He has a massive ego.'**
- **'She'll need a bit more ego to be successful.'**

The Eastern traditions, which go back thousands of years, take a different view. The ego is the *false self*, which makes you see yourself as separate from everyone and everything. You grab as much as you can, while perhaps considering the wellbeing of a few people close to you. The ego is the root of all discrimination, conflict and environmental destruction.

The ego doesn't necessarily make you feel superior to other people – it can also make you feel *inferior*. For example, you might have a pain pattern which says you're unacceptable or unlovable. That's still ego – it makes you feel separate.

In this book, I'm using the Eastern definition of the ego. Completion dissolves the ego, making it irrelevant.

Your ego can destroy your organization

I once conducted a straw poll among investors in early-stage companies. Ninety-five per cent of them agreed with the following statement: 'Most start-ups are destroyed by the founders' egos.' One investor said that companies are also destroyed by investors' egos. I've seen examples of both.

This is part of a general phenomenon. Most people are driven by their root patterns, which I described in chapter 4. They have experiences in their early childhood which are so painful that they *suppress* the pain – instead of experiencing it fully from beginning to end. They also come to conclusions about themselves, other people, the world and life in general. All of this combines to form their ego.

If you try to run your life or lead an organization with your ego then you're setting yourself up for stress and frustration. Since you see yourself as separate you'll soon find yourself trying to manipulate other people using fear and greed. This may appear to work for a short while with a small group. However, as you take responsibility for more people and resources, you'll experience more and more stress. You'll also spread stress and dissatisfaction throughout your organization.

I invite you to stop and reflect on this. You may be running a business, a family, a non-profit organization, or a country. If you try to do so with your mind – or ego – you're heading towards mental overload and an enormous amount of stress.

If you persist with this approach you'll need to keep doing the following:

1. **Anticipate what could go wrong, as well as opportunities you might miss if you aren't prepared for them.**
2. **Anticipate what action other people may take – both within and outside your organization.**
3. **Mentally prepare for each scenario. If there are too many of them, then you may have to figure out which scenarios are most likely to occur and focus on those.**

Even these three steps won't give you peace of mind, because an unexpected event could make some or all of your plans irrelevant. This could happen at any time.

Fortunately, there's an alternative. You can follow the steps I'm describing in this book. Then you'll become blissful and resourceful. Lots of people will want to be with you and follow you. You can explain unclutching, completion and manifestation. You'll experience the fulfilment of enriching a growing number of people around you.

If you're a member of an organization whose leader is in the grip of fear and greed, I recommend you keep completing and unclutching. Remember they're an extension of you. They are you.

At some point something will happen in the world around you. Maybe your boss will change or they'll disappear from your life and be replaced by someone else. Maybe you'll have a new boss in your existing organization or a new boss in another organization. Maybe you'll become your own boss.

These changes may sound disconcerting at first, but if you follow the steps I'm describing in this book, you'll get used to rapid change occurring around you in response to changes in your inner space. You'll be peaceful inside while the world around you rearranges itself.

Let go of expectations

If you have an expectation, you limit what can happen. It's much better to unclutch from any ideas you may have about how things are going to work out. Allow the Cosmic Intelligence to manifest in ways beyond your logic.

Everything is interconnected. When we let go of our expectations, we become open to the beauty of life as it unfolds. We allow the Divine to manifest in ways beyond our imagination.

Everyone is a reflection of you – everyone *is* you

The concept of *projection* is well-known in Western psychology and is often associated with Sigmund Freud and Carl Jung. They saw it as an unconscious mechanism: we attribute our unacceptable thoughts, feelings and desires to other people.

The way you perceive others is a projection of your inner state. A quality you find unacceptable or irritating in other people is a reflection of something you haven't acknowledged or accepted in yourself. If you find other people judgemental, you may look inwards and realize that *you're* judgemental. If you feel that other people are attention-seekers, you may be denying your own craving for attention.

At the deepest level there's no separation between you and other people. They're part of you. Once you start practising completion regularly, it will become easier to observe the pain patterns in the people around you and in the media. Please look inwards. It's likely that you have the same pain patterns.

Once you begin to observe other people's pain patterns – and the effect they're having – you'll have more compassion for them. They're part of you. I'm passing on the tools to help you alleviate their suffering.

As I mentioned earlier in this chapter, when we're complete and unclutched we experience *nirvikalpa samadhi* – unwavering oneness with the source. Then we can experience the Cosmic Intelligence – Paramashiva – manifesting through us.

You'll also begin to experience 'the order in the chaos'.

FALL IN TUNE WITH THE COSMIC ORDER

Many of us complain about chaos – at home, at work, and in the world as a whole. If we keep trying to impose our logic on reality, we're bound to get frustrated. The Cosmic Intelligence is far more sophisticated than our logic.

When we tune into the Cosmic Intelligence, we see there's a beautiful order in the apparent chaos. This happens – for example – when we unclutch and everything falls into place, or when we complete and manifest our desires.

If you read this book and do the exercises, you'll find it much easier to live in tune with the cosmic order.

Don't question the intelligence that's running the cosmos – question your pain patterns

In chapter 6, I described my feeling that something was wrong, which started when I was crying in my cot and nobody came. That was before I had any vocabulary. Now let's fast-forward to the time when we're grown up and can express ourselves in words.

If we say something's wrong in any area of our lives, then we're questioning the Cosmic Intelligence. Our culture is *constantly* doing this. The media keeps highlighting this or that crisis – partly because it's a proven way of getting our attention. The underlying theme is that something is wrong, very wrong.

The belief that something is wrong will keep us stuck. Instead, we should question our pain patterns. Anytime something happens that makes you feel powerless, your patterns are being triggered. This is an opportunity to:

- **Look inwards and listen to yourself.**
- **Identify the pain pattern that's making you feel powerless.**
- **Find the original incident when this pain pattern started.**
- **Re-live the original incident intensely, so the pattern leaves your body.**

Instead of questioning the intelligence that's running the cosmos, we need to question our pain patterns. Once I'd found the original incident and re-lived it intensely, my list of things that weren't working became much shorter. As always, when we work on the inside, the world around us changes.

Everything is auspicious

In addition to seeing ourselves as separate, many of us see our lives as precarious. We label each incident as good or bad. There's a lot of fear.

The Vedic tradition adopts the opposite approach. When we align with the Cosmic Intelligence, we see that everything is being orchestrated for our growth and enlightenment. From that point of view, everything is a blessing. As Swamiji puts it, 'Everything is auspicious.'[11]

Life keeps showing us our pain patterns, so we can complete with them. It also reminds us that we need to surrender to the intelligence that's running the cosmos. Sometimes life does both at the same time.

Surrender doesn't mean you give up – or stop taking action

Surrender means action with an attitude of surrender. We take action without attachment to the results. In the meantime, we relax into the flow.

Earlier, I described my experience in Paris when I surrendered and everything worked out. Since then I've met many people who've had similar experiences. Here's an example from a friend of mine.

'I'd been living in Singapore for four years, having moved there to start the Asia Pacific branch of an executive-search (headhunting) business in the UK. Unfortunately, the market deteriorated and the business closed down. I was left with little money and no job. As a single mother with an eight-year-old daughter, I felt I had to find a way back to the UK.

'I borrowed some money from my sister, who lived in Bali, for our airfare and to ship our items home. She asked us to visit her in Bali for two weeks prior to returning to the UK and sent two air tickets. I decided to tell my daughter of our imminent return. One day after the gym, we were sitting having our breakfast at a café and I prepared her for this forthcoming event. Being an old soul, she told me to stop thinking and talking about returning to England. "If you keep saying this, you'll *think* yourself back to England! Trust in the Universe and stop thinking this!"

'This message from my wise little sage made me sit up and realize that she was right! At some level I felt deep down that I wasn't ready to leave Singapore yet. I didn't know why I felt this, but I did. So that night in my meditation, I asked spirit for guidance and surrendered the situation to the Universe.

'The next morning, the owner of the relocation company that was shipping my home contents to the UK came over to give me a quotation. He was a friend of a friend, a lovely jovial Scottish man who'd been in Singapore for over a decade. In the middle of counting my items, he asked me why I was returning to the UK and what I did for a living. I told him my company had closed down, and that I was in executive search. He then mentioned that he knew two gentlemen at the cricket club who owned an executive-search firm in Singapore and suggested introducing me. I agreed, so he sent an introductory email there and then. When I woke up the next day, I had an email in my inbox asking me if I could call them and come into their office that day for an interview! You can imagine my shock!

'I called one of the partners and told them I was flying out to Bali the next day to visit my sister for two weeks prior to my departure. They insisted I came into the office the same day. I went in and met them and had a great meeting. They were looking for someone with my expertise to set up a new division for them. The next day, I flew to Bali with my daughter and continued with my plans to have my things shipped out on my return and fly back to the UK at the end of that month.

'A week into my time in Bali, I got a phone call from both the partners telling me to cancel my shipment and my flights back to England as they wanted to offer me a job to start immediately on my return to Singapore! I could never have imagined such a turn of events. I realized that, if I surrender to the Universe, miracles can indeed happen!'

As you read this, there may be one or more aspects of your life that aren't working the way you want. From close up it may look like a big problem that's very hard to solve. This is an opportunity to move on from your mind to Cosmic Intelligence.

Maybe you've been making a big effort and getting nowhere. I've experienced that many times. Each time, I was forced to look inwards and change. Then my life changed rapidly for the better.

If you zoom out and look at the situation through the lens of 'everything is auspicious', you'll see it differently. Let's start with the pain patterns that are preventing you from manifesting your desires.

Remember: re-live to relieve

Please write down the answers to these questions:

- How do you feel right now?
- What's your earliest memory of feeling this way? (It may be before the age of seven.)
- Become that age again. What's happening?
- What are your conclusions about yourself, other people, the world and life in general? ('I am . . .', 'People are . . .', 'The world is . . .', 'Life is . . .')

That conclusion is now a belief or pain pattern that's running your life. It's time to re-live the original incident to relieve it.

Please re-live that early incident intensely, at least five times with your eyes closed and at least five times talking to yourself in a mirror. You may suddenly recall an even earlier incident. Please re-live that one in the same way. Keep going, back to the root.

If you complete with the pain pattern that's being triggered in this situation, it will help you to manifest your desires in any area of your life. It could even happen immediately. (Remember my folding bicycle?)

Applying the completion technique will dramatically reduce your pain patterns and the negative thoughts they generate. Your thoughts will fall towards zero. Then you'll see the immediate possibilities that life is showing you.

Then you can embrace each moment with enthusiasm and fully experience the present. You let go of your resistance and surrender to the intelligence that's running the cosmos. You become open to abundance and fulfilment in all aspects of your life.

GRATITUDE IS THE HIGHEST STATE OF CONSCIOUSNESS

When we shift our focus from what we lack to what we have, our emotional state changes and we move to higher states of consciousness. Then we manifest our desires much more easily.

You may have noticed by now that some of your desires are manifesting with little or no thought on your part. When you notice this – as I often do – say 'thank you', either silently or out loud. You'll become increasingly conscious that you're manifesting your desires, ranging from apparently small things to very big things. In terms of your spiritual growth, it doesn't matter how big or small you perceive each manifestation to be. The point is, you're manifesting your desires.

In my case, even suicidal depression now looks like a blessing. Let's go back to the metaphor of the hundred-storey building which illustrates the levels of consciousness. When I was clinically depressed, I was in the basement, in the dark. There were few if any helpful coincidences. I felt separate from everyone and everything. Since learning and applying the principles I'm sharing in this book, I've moved upwards and experience helpful coincidences frequently. Things keep falling into place, often in unexpected, beautiful ways.

Cultivate gratitude

We can cultivate gratitude for so many things:

- **Our bodies**
- **The food we eat**
- **The furniture we sit on**
- **The people around us**
- **The things people do for us**
- **The fact we're still breathing**

When we're conscious of the blessings being showered on us, we're more aware of the benevolence of Existence, God, or whatever you want to call it.

Our final chapter will show what happens when we surrender and tune into this intelligence.

Let go of your expectations and be grateful for what's happening now

Please take a pen and an exercise book or pad of paper. Make a list of everything for which you can be grateful.

You may notice some changes when you do this:

- When we do our work with some kind of expectation, there's a subtle violence in our body language: the way we type on the keyboard, the way we move around, the way we talk to people. When we're grateful we let go of that violence.

- When we experience deep gratitude, our body language changes. We start flowing with Existence. We move gracefully.

- We enjoy what we're doing, without expecting a particular result.

Be grateful for whatever happens. Even painful experiences can be a blessing. They're showing us how we need to grow spiritually – and manifest more easily.

SUMMARY

- We have two options: to keep analysing and solving each problem that comes up, or to surrender to the intelligence that's running the cosmos. That intelligence will then manifest through you and fulfil your desires.
- If you become a pure channel, the Cosmic Intelligence can manifest anything through you.
- It's best to leave the timing to the cosmos.
- According to the Eastern traditions, the ego is the *false self*. It makes you see yourself as separate from everyone and everything.
- The ego doesn't necessarily make you feel superior to other people. It can also make you feel *inferior*.
- Completion dissolves the ego, making it irrelevant and preventing it from destroying your organization.
- If you have an expectation, you limit what can happen.
- When we tune into the Cosmic Intelligence, we see there's a beautiful order in the apparent chaos.
- Everything is auspicious.
- Surrender doesn't mean you give up – or stop taking action.
- Gratitude is the highest state of consciousness, in which our desires manifest much more easily.

8

ASK THE COSMIC INTELLIGENCE TO MANIFEST THROUGH YOU

In the last chapter, I described two options in life. The first is to keep analysing every situation and potential course of action, the second is to surrender to the intelligence that's running the cosmos. That intelligence will then manifest through you and fulfil your true desires, which I described in chapter 1. You may be wondering why the Cosmic Intelligence would fulfil your desires, instead of doing something else.

Most Western-educated people have been brought up to believe that God is either separate from them or non-existent. By contrast, the Vedic tradition says we're all divine.

In this chapter I'll show you how to align your consciousness with the cosmos. I began to experience this regularly when I started asking the Cosmic Intelligence – known as Paramashiva in the Vedic tradition – to manifest through me.

In the second year of the Covid pandemic, I travelled on my own for ten days in South Wales, around 200 miles west of London. I ended up in Pembrokeshire, a beautiful county where there's a lot to see and not much accommodation or public transport.

Having talked to people in the county town of Pembroke, I realized I would need a car to see everything I wanted to see. I called the well-known car-hire firms, one of which said they had a car available. It was expensive, but I agreed. A few minutes later they called back to say that someone else had taken it. As they say in India, 'What to do?'

I knew that getting powerless and frustrated wasn't going to help, so I unclutched. I kept calling on the Cosmic Intelligence to manifest through me. I kept saying inwardly, 'Paramashiva, please manifest through me.' I called one of the big-name car-hire firms again, in case they had any cancellations. The lady who answered the phone said no, then recommended a local firm 15 minutes' walk from where I was staying. The only vehicle they had available was an eight-seater van, which was much cheaper to hire than the cars I'd been considering. The fuel was also cheaper because it ran on diesel. I put my rucksack in the big van and drove to Curlew Castle, then St David's Cathedral.

If you've ever travelled with no reservations, you'll know that you keep finding yourself in situations where there's no obvious solution. For me it was a great opportunity to try this new approach. Over and over again I said, 'Paramashiva, please manifest through me.' When I returned to Pembroke that evening, I searched online and found a place to stay – a room in a small house in Tenby. I also wanted to wash my clothes after several days of travel – but had no idea where I could do so. I booked the room and drove to Tenby. While I was finding my way through the narrow streets in my eight-seater van, my mind was nagging me about where I was going to park. I kept saying to myself, 'Paramashiva, please manifest through me.'

Eventually I realized I was close to the house, which was on a busy road with no parking. Suddenly I noticed a large builders' truck parked in a side street. The builders were loading it up to go home for the night. One of them walked across the street and said to me, 'You can have our parking space.' I parked the van and walked towards the house. It turned out to be next door to a laundromat – where I washed my clothes that evening.

The Cosmic Intelligence can synchronize everything

While I was writing this book I received an invitation to a partners' meeting in Singapore. It was a long way from London, but I realized that I'd also have the opportunity to meet a friend who lived there.

The partners' meeting was then moved from Singapore to Dubai. I felt frustrated, but at least the flight was shorter. I shelved the idea of meeting my friend and carried on asking Paramashiva to manifest through me.

While I was in Dubai I wanted to make a short trip to Riyadh to meet a potential client and the Arabic publisher of my earlier book, *The Power of Letting Go*. My colleagues told me it would only take a few minutes to get a visa online. However, it took me far longer.

With the help of my colleagues I solved one technical problem after another. I kept saying inwardly, 'Paramashiva, please manifest through me.'

I completed all the technical steps and obtained my Saudi visa three days later than planned. In the meantime I fulfilled a longstanding desire to visit Ras Al Khaimah – a bus ride north of Dubai.

While all of this was going on, I was in touch with my friend, who'd been travelling in Africa. He was about to return to Singapore – via Dubai. I realized that if I took the 2am flight from Dubai to Riyadh, then he and I could meet in Dubai Airport at midnight, which we did. The end result was that three of my desires were fulfilled simultaneously – in an unexpected way:

1. **I visited Ras Al Khaimah**
2. **I met a potential client and my Arabic publisher in Riyadh**
3. **I met my friend from Singapore.**

I've noticed that, when I unclutch and ask Paramashiva to manifest through me, I don't feel afraid anymore. I accept what's happening and remain present. It isn't my job to figure out how my desires are going to be realized, so I'm no longer plagued by a feeling of impossibility. All I have to do is keep unclutching, surrendering. Then I know what I need to do next – and I do it. I spend little time thinking about the past. Instead, I look forwards. I move on.

If we surrender we can handle any situation

Shortly after my trip to Dubai and Saudi Arabia, three things happened in the space of a few weeks. My landlord gave me two months' notice to move out of the apartment. My girlfriend moved back to her home country – I never saw her again. Then my mum fell on the floor in her care home and broke her hip. She had an operation and left the body three days later. While helping to organize the funeral I visited 15 apartments and made three offers, all of which were rejected.

Back in the days when I relied on my mind to solve problems, this situation would have been extremely stressful, with a flood of negative emotions. Fortunately, I was already declaring powerful cognitions such as 'Paramashiva is manifesting through me'.

Throughout each day I kept saying inwardly, 'Paramashiva, please manifest through me.' Then I unclutched. Everything worked smoothly, with little worry or stress. In the days leading up to my mum's passing, our family was in the hospital with her. The following day, I returned to London with only two weeks to go before I had to move out of my apartment. Then an agent showed me a suitable apartment which had just been put on the market at a discount. I made an offer which was immediately accepted. Everything went smoothly, with little worry or stress.

Things work out much better if you surrender

My earlier book, *The Power of Letting Go*, was published in the US the day the bookshops closed at the start of the Covid pandemic. I unclutched and kept going, without any expectations about the results.

Having read the book, some people started contacting me, asking if they could interview me for their podcasts. Then sales accelerated. *The Power of Letting Go* has already sold ten times more than my earlier book, *Brand You*.

Instead of constantly trying to figure out what will happen and what we need to do about it, we can move on: we ask the intelligence that's running the cosmos to run our lives. This removes doubt and frustration. Life keeps unfolding and things keep happening, with little or no stress.

Sometimes people say to me, 'I can't go on any longer' or 'I can't go on like this.' I find that very encouraging. It's a sign that they're close to dropping their ego – the little 'I' – and surrendering. If they surrender, everything will work out for them. The simplest way to surrender is to unclutch and ask the Cosmic Intelligence to manifest through you.

When we surrender and take action, we become a channel for the Divine. There's a famous verse in the *Bhagavad Gita* in which Krishna says to Arjuna, 'Never consider yourself to be the cause of the results of your activities.'[12]

Surrender is a profound concept that transcends our ordinary understanding. It's not about giving up. It's about recognizing a higher power and allowing the Divine to flow through us. When we surrender, we trust the Cosmic Intelligence. We open ourselves to receive guidance, wisdom and blessings. We let go of the burden of trying to control what happens. We allow the Divine to take charge of our lives.

Surrender may seem like an alien concept at first, particularly if you were brought up as an atheist, or in a religion that tried to control you. Many of us are afraid of allowing the Cosmic Intelligence to run our lives, until we realize that it's *inside us*. As Swamiji says, 'I'm not here to convince you that I am God. I'm here to convince you that you are God.'

If you keep completing and unclutching, your mind will become quieter and quieter. It will become increasingly obvious that you're consciousness. You aren't the chaotic thoughts – or your body – which keep changing.

I invite you to let go of the habit of constantly analysing the situation and trying to solve problems by thinking a lot. Instead, ask the intelligence that's running the cosmos to manifest through you. That's when the magic happens.

There's a famous quotation from Sri Ramana Maharshi, an enlightened master who lived in India.[13] He said, 'He who thinks he is the doer is also the sufferer.' In other words, if you think your body/mind is making things happen, then you're always going to suffer. If you understand that Supreme Consciousness is manifesting through you, you can welcome it and relax.

As always, 'If you surrender, your intuition will tell you what to do.' You may find yourself taking lots of action, but it will be with an attitude of surrender. You can relax and enjoy life as it happens in and around you.

Ask to be guided

You may recall that, when I was living in Paris – broke and ill – I let go completely and asked to be guided. A few days later, the perfect job appeared in the newspaper. While you're looking for your pain patterns or the original incidents, you can also ask to be guided. As Jesus said in the Sermon on the Mount, 'Ask and you shall receive.'

One of my friends read a draft of this book and was making great progress with completion. When I asked her what she was doing, she said she'd asked Paramashiva to show her. That's exactly what I did when I identified the original painful incidents that I described in chapter 4.

You can do the same. You can ask the Cosmic Intelligence to show you your pain patterns and the incidents when you came to those conclusions. Imagine you're standing in a very large train station and need some information. The quickest way to get it is to ask someone in the information booth.

Make your root pattern redundant

For a while I thought my root pattern must be related to my experience at the age of one, when I was crying in my cot but nobody came. I concluded that something was wrong.

However, it dawned on me that this couldn't be my root pattern, because I didn't have any vocabulary at that age. You can't come to a conclusion about yourself, other people, the world or life in general if you don't have any words to express it!

I realized that the earliest painful incident when I came to conclusions was at the age of three when my mum made me have my hair cut. I felt powerless and concluded something along the lines of 'I'm a powerless victim. Life doesn't give me what I want.'

Now that I was clear about the root incident, I re-lived it intensely again – over and over again with my eyes closed and talking to myself in the mirror. There was a lot more detail than when I'd re-lived it previously. I saw the light streaming through the windows into an area with a wooden floor and lots of wooden furniture. The barber was wearing a white shirt, with his black hair slicked back. There were also smells – his strong, musty aftershave, and the Brylcreem in his hair.

Over the next few days I made several observations:

- **My mind was much quieter. There were few thoughts about the past or the future.**
- **I had to concentrate to remember my root pattern, which had become redundant.**
- **When I turned inwards, there was an empty space, with very little commentary running in the background – unlike before.**
- **Things began to manifest much more easily.**
- **I need to be very careful what I wish for. Anything I hold in my inner space will manifest.**

Our incompletions are like a tree with deep roots and lots of branches. Making my patterns redundant feels like pulling up the tree and leaving it lying on the ground. I can still see it if I look down.

The earth around the roots is the feeling that something's wrong. Then there's my root pattern: 'I'm a powerless victim' and 'Life doesn't give me what I want'. There are several main branches: 'I'm unacceptable', 'I'm a failure', 'It isn't fair', 'It's impossible'. There are lots of smaller branches, such as 'People keep telling me what to do'. There are also a few twigs: painful incidents in the recent past which I haven't completed yet.

So much for the tree. Now that it's lying on the ground, it doesn't block the view when I look straight ahead. It's redundant, irrelevant.

I updated my chart, which now looks like this:

Incident	Age	Conclusions/pain patterns running my life ever since					
In the barber's chair, being forced to have my hair cut	3	'I'm a powerless victim'	'Life doesn't give me what I want'				
Children laughing at my accent on my first day at school	5	'I'm a powerless victim'	'Life doesn't give me what I want'	'I'm unacceptable'	'It isn't fair'		
Failing the colour-blindness test, which meant I couldn't fly planes	6	'I'm a powerless victim'	'Life doesn't give me what I want'	'I'm unacceptable'	'It isn't fair'	'I'm a failure'	'It's impossible'

How about you?

I encourage you to create your own pain-pattern chart. It really helps to put everything down on paper, so you can see what's going on and complete with the patterns that are running your life. You're likely to produce several drafts – as I have. It's all part of the process.

I'm helping you to discover and complete with your pain patterns

From then on I started helping people to do two things:

1. **Identify the five or six pain patterns that are running their lives – and the original incidents when they came to those conclusions about themselves, other people, the world and life in general.**
2. **Identify and complete with their root pattern, which is the root of their suffering and prevents them from manifesting their desires.**

A couple of weeks later I woke up with the realization that everything is possible. I'd heard people say this many times before, but now I understood why it's true:

- **We're consciousness. Whatever we hold in our inner space manifests in our bodies and all around us.**
- **Once our root pattern becomes redundant, there's little or nothing stopping our true desires from manifesting.**
- **If we unclutch and surrender to the intelligence that's running the cosmos, our intuition tells us what to do.**

You may experience intuition as a thought, a feeling, a vision, an instruction or even a sound. As I mentioned, your incompletions can give rise to false intuition. It's therefore essential to complete with any pain pattern that comes to your attention.

If you surrender, your intuition will tell you what to do.

Experience more love

As I said in the introduction, most of us have been conditioned to believe that we're separate from other people. This means that, if we want to experience love, we have to look outside ourselves. It's a common theme in our culture – including literature, opera and pop songs. People always seem to be looking for love, finding it and losing it again.

You are love. It's your nature. The more you complete with your pain patterns, the more love will pour out of you. You will naturally help people, take care of them, and do whatever you can to alleviate their suffering. Instead of judging them, you'll have compassion and a desire to help them remove their own pain patterns.

At some point you may notice that more and more people want to be around you. They're attracted by your inner space. It all starts with completion. If you're in the space of completion, you'll radiate and attract love.

SUMMARY

- Surrender is the state in which the individual will is aligned with the cosmic will.
- The Cosmic Intelligence can synchronize everything; things fall into place.
- If you surrender, you'll be able to handle any situation that arises with little or no stress. Things work out much better if we surrender.
- Once your root pattern becomes redundant, there's little or nothing stopping your desires from manifesting.
- If you surrender, your intuition will tell you what to do.
- If you're in the space of completion, you'll radiate and attract love.

CONCLUSION

The starting point for most of us is that we see ourselves as separate body/minds. Then we think a lot, in an attempt to get what we want and avoid what we don't want. Many of us fall into the trap of constantly analysing ourselves and our situation. We feel more and more separate – and possibly depressed.

Once we understand we're consciousness, we realize there's no separation. We experience this particularly when we serve others. We attract more and more resources and supporters. We feel fulfilled and experience abundance.

These days I focus on enriching everyone around me. Swamiji says that 'Enriching others is not about seeking recognition or rewards; it is about selflessly contributing to their growth as part of your own journey.' You can do the same. Here are some examples:

- **Helping someone to find their pain patterns and complete with them.**
- **Sharing the unclutching technique with anyone who's struggling with negative thoughts and emotions.**
- **Passing on a useful idea, contact or piece of information.**

This may sound like hard work at first, but it really isn't – and consider the benefits:

- **If the people around you learn to complete and unclutch, it will raise the level of their consciousness. It will be easier for all of you to manifest your desires – and fulfil your potential.**
- **I often do something to help someone, and forget about it. Sometimes it leads to a new friendship, a new experience or a business opportunity, for example.**

Serving others will give you the experience of oneness: your connection with others and the whole universe.

This book is like a guide to a country you've never visited. I hope you've enjoyed reading about it. Whether you go there is up to you.

I encourage you to do the exercises and apply these five principles in your daily life:

1. **Listen to yourself and others**
2. **Complete**
3. **Unclutch**
4. **Ask the Cosmic Intelligence to manifest through you**
5. **Be grateful**

If you keep doing this, the intelligence that runs the cosmos will run your life and take care of your desires. Enjoy!

20 TIPS FOR MANIFESTING

1. Keep your living and working spaces clean and tidy

This is good for your inner space, where you hold your desires until they manifest.

I encourage you to:

- **Look around you. Is there something you don't enjoy looking at – or don't use on a regular basis? If so, clean it and store it out of sight, give it away or sell it.**
- **Tidy the contents of any drawers. Again, if there are items you don't use, you can store them, give them away or sell them.**
- **Tidy your bookshelf (if you have one), your sock drawer and the clothing in your wardrobe and cupboards.**

You're creating space for something new.

2. Micromanage your money

You may not be conscious of what's happening with your wealth – and your money in particular.

Here's a simple exercise:

- **Every night, check your bank account on your mobile phone or other device. Take a pen and a sheet of paper. In the left-hand column, make a list of any money that's come in today.**
- **In the right-hand column, make a list of what you spent today, either because you chose to or because you have some automated payment running in the background.**

As you become more aware of the money flowing in and out, you'll become more conscious of your decisions and actions.

(Am I really spending that much on chocolate? How much is that per year?)

You'll also see the effect of incompletions or pain patterns on your finances. What are you spending money on, in an attempt to feel better? What's the pain pattern driving this behaviour? What's the original incident when you came to this conclusion about yourself, other people, the world or life in general? Please complete it now.

3. Don't overload your memory

I find it helpful to keep my to-do list and shopping list on my phone – which synchronizes with my laptop. Then I don't need to remember lots of details. This makes manifestation easier.

4. Manage your inner space

If you keep practising completion, you'll feel excited and inspired.

Remember that whatever you carry in your inner space will start manifesting in and around you. Avoid watching or listening to violence.

5. Practise yoga

Yoga means 'union'. It unites you with your inner self and the Divine. Practising yoga in the traditional way prepares your body, mind and soul for oneness with the cosmic energy,[14] allowing it to flow through you effortlessly.

You can set an intention – or *sankalpa* – at the beginning of each yoga session, for whatever you want to manifest.

6. Connect with nature

When we spend time in nature we become more conscious of the intelligence that's running the cosmos, including our bodies and everything around us.

7. Listen to yourself

Most of us rush around trying to solve the problems that keep appearing in our lives without realizing that we manifested them in the first place. We also react compulsively to the thoughts that appear in our inner space. Our reactions range from overeating to depression, anger and even physical violence.

If you sit and listen to yourself:

- **You'll discover the thought patterns that are manifesting in your body and all around you.**
- **You'll see what's going on inside you, including any desire to do something.**
- **You can look for signals in your body. What are they telling you?**
- **You'll see if you've suppressed some desire or painful experience.**
- **You'll know how to respond to life.**

I encourage you to sit with a pen and a pad of paper. Listen to yourself carefully. Write it all down.

8. Love yourself

Many of us have been told this, but we don't know how to do it.

Here are some steps to help you cultivate love for yourself:

1. **Celebrate yourself: Acknowledge your unique qualities and the great things that have happened in your life so far. Celebrate your uniqueness without comparison to others.**
2. **Have compassion for yourself: Treat yourself with kindness, especially at times when you find life difficult. Remember that it's okay to make mistakes. They're part of your growth.**
3. **Take care of yourself: Prioritize activities that nourish your body, mind and spirit. These include healthy eating, exercise and hobbies that bring you joy.**
4. **Forgive yourself: Let go of any grievances and forgive yourself for what you perceive as mistakes. Embrace the lessons you learned from those experiences.**
5. **Surround yourself with positivity: Spend time with people who uplift and support you.**

If you practise these steps consistently, you'll cultivate love and acceptance of yourself. You'll allow that love to radiate into the world.

You attract what you radiate. If you radiate love and peace, you'll naturally attract people and situations that resonate with those qualities.

9. Use your successes as stepping stones to future success

If you focus on your successes and feel grateful, you'll raise the level of your consciousness. Don't compare yourself with others. Take the time to do things right, instead of rushing things. Don't worry about results. Just focus on what you're doing, and do it to the best of your ability.

10. Visualize your desire, instead of constantly analysing

Many of us are in the habit of analysing the situation and trying to solve one problem after another. The mind then produces reasons why things are the way they are, and why something hasn't happened yet. If we keep engaging with the mind, we start to hold onto these reasons. If you start believing in reasons why something hasn't happened or can't happen, then you start manifesting obstacles.

It's much better to keep visualizing your desire as already manifested. Then it will start to become reality. You'll keep having ideas for things you can do and people you can contact to make it happen. Keep taking action until it manifests.

11. Close your eyes and focus

It's easy to be distracted by what you see happening around you. The current situation can also trigger your pain patterns if you haven't fully completed with them. The solution is to close your eyes for a short while and focus on two things:

1. **Any powerful cognitions that are in your inner space.**
2. **The desire that you're manifesting.**

Remember that whatever you carry in your inner space will start manifesting in your body and all around you.

12. Unclutch and move out of your comfort zone

When we're about to do something new, we may experience fear, greed or uncertainty. If we unclutch from all that, we can move out of our comfort zone. We don't know the outcome, but we still take action. Then things start happening. When we unclutch we feel a connection with the ecosystem around us, which supports us.

Before I learned completion and unclutching I was very choosy about who I spoke to. My pain patterns severely limited my interactions with other people. These days I'll talk to practically anyone. When I unclutch and move out of my comfort zone, I see how the situation changes and everything falls into place.

13. Treat every situation as new

The longer we spend on planet Earth, the more experiences we have. We tend to accumulate opinions about people, situations, words, actions, looks and gestures. Some of our opinions take the form of generalizations. Please note:

- **Opinions block our connection with life, which is continually unfolding.**
- **When our view is clouded by opinions, we don't even see what's going on.**
- **When we're highly opinionated we end up working from memory.**
- **Our creativity is replaced by opinions, which stop us from manifesting.**
- **When we're full of opinions we miss opportunities.**

Let go of your opinions

Please take a pen and a piece of paper. Make a list of your opinions. Some will have come from your experiences. Others may have been imposed on you by society. I invite you to let go of them. Then you'll start to see things as they are and treat every situation as new.

14. Let go of judgements

Many of us judge what's happening as good or bad. This creates stress and frustration. We're resisting what is.

I invite you to drop the habit of judging. It will help you to flow with life. Your desires will manifest more easily. As William Shakespeare wrote in his play *Hamlet*, 'There is nothing either good or bad, but thinking makes it so.'

I'm not saying you should ignore what's going on around you, or simply allow others to suffer. I'm saying that judgements don't help. For example, if someone is doing something that's likely to cause suffering, you can point it out to them. There's no need to judge or label them. That will only create more resistance.

15. Find one solution to many problems

Most of us see ourselves as separate and think a lot, so we approach problems with fear and greed. We worry about what may or may not happen – and what people will say. We're afraid of being misunderstood. We also point fingers at other people. We try to manipulate *them* using fear and greed. If we carry on like this we'll face one problem after another. It's exhausting.

If you stand back and look at the situation, you'll see that one pain pattern is creating multiple problems. For example, if you believe you can't trust anyone, this will show up in your personal and professional life. You're likely to find yourself surrounded by people who don't trust you either. They're reflecting your blind spot: your lack of trust in other people.

Your problems are a reflection of your pain patterns. If you look inwards and complete with the pattern that's causing one problem, other problems will be solved simultaneously.

In this example, the lack of trust in your personal and professional life can be resolved if you identify the original incident when you concluded that 'I can't trust anyone'. Please re-live the original incident intensely, as I described in chapter 4. You'll know you've completed when your situation changes for the better.

16. If you make your root pattern redundant, you'll see things as they are

Your mind filters experiences through your root pattern. You judge what you perceive and then assemble selected pieces to support your judgement.

If you discover your root pattern, complete with it and make it redundant, you'll see things as they are. This is a huge advantage in every aspect of life.

17. Give the best

The principle of *Advaita* – or oneness – applies to everything we do. If you give the best to yourself and others you'll attract the best things from the cosmos.

To put it another way, the cosmos gives back what you're radiating. When you give the best, you'll attract the best in life.

18. Become aware of your breath

If you become aware of your breath you can remain in the present. This reduces stress and enhances your overall wellbeing.

Mindfulness of breathing is a great way to start. Simply place your attention on your breath as it flows in and out of your body. Every time your attention wanders, bring it back to the breath.

19. Become aware of your actions

If we aren't careful, our responses to life become repetitive. We become insensitive to what's happening and are less and less conscious of what we're doing. We may find ourselves repeating mistakes. We become robotic rather than creative.

Once you're aware of your breath, you can extend your awareness to the sensations in your body and what's going on around you. You'll also become aware of your actions.

20. Don't get dragged into other people's dramas

Now that you know about pain patterns and completion, you can follow this situation as it unfolds:

- **Sonia has an experience which triggers one of her pain patterns. She feels powerless.**
- **Sonia now says or does something which triggers one of Adam's pain patterns.**
- **Now Adam feels powerless and reacts to what Sonia has just said or done.**

You can see this kind of drama playing out in businesses, families, voluntary organizations and many other situations.

Adam's reaction is likely to be one of four well-known trauma responses:

Fight: Adam argues with Sonia.

Flight: Adam runs away from Sonia.

Freeze: Adam does nothing.

Fawn: Adam tries to please Sonia, and avoid conflict with her.

In each case, little or nothing gets done.

If Sonia and Adam look inwards and complete with their pain patterns, this whole drama will stop. They're unlikely to do that – most people aren't conscious of their patterns.

You can just watch and listen. There's no need to get dragged into the drama. It's like watching tennis at Wimbledon. I call it *trauma tennis.* Once Sonia and Adam are exhausted, you can help them to complete with their pain patterns.

REFERENCES

1. The full title of Sir Isaac Newton's groundbreaking work is *Philosophiae Naturalis Principia Mathematica*. His own first edition – in Latin – is on permanent display in the Wren Library at Trinity College, Cambridge, England. It contains his handwritten corrections for the second edition.
2. Paramashiva can be translated as 'causeless auspiciousness'.
3. Ken Roberts, *A Rich Man's Secret: An Amazing Formula for Success* (Llewellyn Publications, 1995)
4. Eckhart Tolle, *The Power of Now: A Guide to Spiritual Enlightenment* (New World Library, 2010)
5. Transcendental Meditation – see *www.tm.org*. Another helpful resource is Norman E Rosenthal, *Transcendence: Healing and Transformation Through Transcendental Meditation* (Penguin, 2011).
6. *Advaita* is sometimes translated as 'non-duality' (see page 190 [Glossary]).
7. Becky Walsh, *You Do Know: Learning to Act on Intuition Instantly* (Hay House, 2013)
8. Srinivasa Ramanujan was born in Erode, India, in 1887. He published his first paper in 1911 and obtained a research scholarship at the University of Madras. In 1914 he moved to Trinity College, Cambridge, where he collaborated with his mentor, GH Hardy. In 1918 he became a fellow of the Royal Society and was then offered a fellowship at Trinity. Suffering from ill health he returned to India in 1919, and died in 1920. Some of Ramanujan's papers are held by the Wren Library at Trinity College, Cambridge.
9. The original source of the completion technique is the ShivaJnana Upanishad, Vijnana Bhairava Tantra, 94th verse, 22nd technique.
10. *Bhagavad Gita* verse 2.48
11. Paramahamsa Nithyananda, *Living Enlightenment*, seventh edition, November 2009, page 189

12. *Bhagavad Gita* verse 2.47. For a step-by-step guide to attaining enlightenment through the timeless teachings of Lord Krishna, see Paramahamsa Nithyananda, *Bhagavad Gita Decoded* (Nithyananda University, 2015).
13. Tiruvannamalai is a prominent pilgrimage destination in Tamil Nadu, India. The Arunachaleshwara Temple to Lord Shiva is located at the base of Arunachala Hill. The *samadhi* (tomb) of Sri Ramana Maharshi (1879–1950) is in Ramanashram in Tiruvannamalai. SPH Sri Nithyananda Paramashivam (Swamiji) was born in Tiruvannamalai in 1978. He spent six months in Ramanashram.
14. 'Cosmic energy' is another term for Paramashiva, the ultimate consciousness.

SPH SRI NITHYANANDA PARAMASHIVAM

I first met Swamiji in 2014, in his ashram near Bangalore, India. 'SPH' stands for 'Supreme Pontiff of Hinduism' (Pontiff means 'bridge-builder'). He's described as an avatar or incarnation – an enlightened being who comes down to lead humanity to enlightenment, as Krishna and others have done before.

GLOSSARY OF SANSKRIT TERMS

Sanskrit is an Indo-European language, which means that Western-educated people can decipher some of it:

Advaita: 'not two' or 'non-dual'. *A-* means 'not' while *dva* means 'two', as it does in Russian and other Slavic languages (like *deux* in French). *Advaita* is a key principle in Advaita Vedanta, a school of Hinduism that emphasizes the oneness of ultimate reality (Brahman).

Asana: a posture in yoga. The Sanskrit word *asana* means 'sitting position' or 'seat', and is related to the French word *assis*, which means 'sitting'.

Bhagavad Gita: 'The Song of the Lord'. *Bhagavad* means 'of the Lord', while *Gita* means 'song'.

Chidakasha: 'consciousness space'. *Chit* means 'consciousness', while *akasha* means 'space'.

Darshan: an opportunity to see a holy person. From *darshana* meaning 'sight' or 'seeing'.

Nithyananda: 'eternal bliss'. *Nithya* means 'eternal', while *ananda* means 'bliss'.

Poornatva: the state of being complete or whole. *Poorna* means 'full' or 'complete'. The suffix *-tva* indicates a quality or state.

Tathastu: 'So be it'. *Tatha* means 'so' or 'thus', while *astu* means 'let it be'.

Veda: (Sacred) knowledge, wisdom.

Yoga: 'Union'. From the Sanskrit root *yuj*, meaning 'to join', 'to yoke' or 'to unite'.

ACKNOWLEDGEMENTS

Ameer Ali, Shamash Alidina, Luis Arsenio, Ma Nithya Atmadayananda, Nell Axelrod, Jonathan Baker, Adam Bennett, André Berry, Patricia Bidi, Michael Blatz, Dr Peter Bloomfield, Alistair Brown, Jacq Burns, Markella Christie, Naomi Courtenay, Anhtuan Do, Dr Barbara Edlmair, Nui Elworthy, Paul Freud, Concetta Gallotta, Sean Gardiner, Mahdieh Ghasemi, Ma Nithya Maha Govindananda, Rajesh Gupta, Michael Hartz, Atif Hasan, Melinda Alexander Haseth, Dr Karishma Hemmady, Camille James, Sumit Jamuar, Ma Nithya Jnanavigrahanda, Sasha Knott, Rupert Konstam, Jeremy Lewis, Cecilia Li, Philip Loy, Michael Maeder, Jeremy Marshall, Elvis Mazija, Petra Miskov, Dr Nitish Mital, Vijaya Neha, Kemi Nejo, Nuno Carvalho, Mark O'Sullivan, Anjali Ozer, Sudha Oza, Marina Paganucci, Tim Payne, David Peto, Mark Phoenix, Elena Pitzk, Roger Purkiss, Simon Purkiss, Carilyn Quigley, Marisha Ray, Anita Rolls, Dr Norman Rosenthal, Mark Rothera, David Royston-Lee, Joe Salem, Jay Shah, Sanjay Shah, Kerstin Shamma'a, Faith Sharp, Bo Shi, Zhen Shi, Dr Rabia Shirazi, Matthew Stafford, Victoria Stead, Steve Swindon, Sharan Kaur Varaitch, Vasantha Viththiyakaran, Karen E Watson, John Williams, Roger Wilson, Adèle Winkeley.

NOTES

NOTES

NOTES

NOTES

NOTES

NOTES

NOTES

ABOUT THE AUTHOR

John Purkiss studied economics at Cambridge University and has an MBA (Master of Business Administration) from INSEAD. He began his career in banking and management consultancy, in London and Chicago, and worked in sales and marketing in the UK and Continental Europe. John then learned to meditate, which made his intuition much stronger and enabled him to move into executive search. He has recruited senior executives and board members for a wide range of companies. John has also invested in high-growth technology companies.

For more details visit his website at www.johnpurkiss.com

Dear Reader,

We'd love your attention for one more page to tell you about the crisis in children's reading, and what we can all do.

Studies have shown that reading for fun is the **single biggest predictor of a child's future success** – more than family circumstance, parents' educational background or income. It improves academic results, mental health, wealth, communication skills and ambition.

The number of children reading for fun is in rapid decline. Young people have a lot of competition for their time, and a worryingly high number do not have a single book at home.

Our business works extensively with schools, libraries and literacy charities, but here are some ways we can all raise more readers:

- Reading to children for just 10 minutes a day makes a difference
- Don't give up if your children aren't regular readers – there will be books for them!
- Visit bookshops and libraries to get recommendations
- Encourage them to listen to audiobooks
- Support school libraries
- Give books as gifts

Thank you for reading.
www.JoinRaisingReaders.com